RelateAbility™

Working Together To Make Work Life Better℠

Ted Malley &
Wade A. McNair, Psy.D.

Technics Publications

BASKING RIDGE, NEW JERSEY

Published by:

TECHNICS PUBLICATIONS

TECHNOLOGY / LEADERSHIP

2 Lindsley Road
Basking Ridge, NJ 07920 USA

https://www.TechnicsPub.com

Cover design by Lorena Molinari
Edited by Sadie Hoberman and Jessica Lakritz

First Printing 2017

ISBN, print ed.	9781634622608
ISBN, Kindle ed.	9781634622615
ISBN, ePub ed.	9781634622622
ISBN, PDF ed.	9781634622639

Library of Congress Control Number: 2017949256

Contents

CONTENTS

Acknowledgements

- A thank you to Dr. Michael Williamson and Dr. Mark Vickers who created the original Communication Styles and Core Convictions that form the foundation of WorkTraits, which later became our TeamRelate Model.

- Additional thanks to Dr. Bart Weathington, Dr. Brian O'Leary, and Dr. Kate Rogers from the University of Tennessee, Chattanooga for assistance in the validation and statistical studies relating to the TeamRelate Survey.

- Special thanks to Gabe Pham-Xuan, M.A., for his exhaustive research and academic support. You are very much appreciated and this book is better because you were involved in the project.

- Our appreciation to Steve Hoberman, our publisher, for his guidance and support in making our dream of publishing into the reality of the book you now hold.

- And finally, much love to the Malley and McNair families. Your unconditional love and support of our work is beyond measure. Your patience and

ACKNOWLEDGEMENTS

understanding as we embark on this incredible
journey is very much appreciated. xoxo

About the Authors

Ted Malley

Mr. Malley has over 25 years of experience as a senior executive in the technology industry and over 20 of those years in the Human Capital Management software business. As the Chief Customer Officer at Ceridian, Mr. Malley combines his personal passion for helping people and for technology to change the way Ceridian loves its customers through their award-winning XOXO Customer Success program.

Before joining Ceridian, Mr. Malley co-founded RelatedMatters, Inc. and developed the mobile app TeamRelate, which was acquired by Ceridian in March 2015. TeamRelate combines mobile technology, social networking, and behavioral science into a powerful communication team-engagement tool for today's workforce. Prior to that, Mr. Malley served at Ultimate Software for 17 years in a variety of positions: VP Customer Relationship Management and General Manager, VP Technology and Product Strategy, and Chief Information Officer. Mr. Malley holds a degree in Computer Science from Cal Poly, San Luis Obispo, CA and loves spending time with his wife and four children in Arroyo Grande, CA.

His personal mission is to work with great teams of people who are driven by achievement, not money, and excellence over status and title. His desire is to change the world for the better, one relationship at a time.

Wade A. McNair, Psy.D.

Dr. McNair is a dynamic Coach, Consultant, and Communicator with over 20 years of experience in Talent Management, Corporate Learning, Leadership, Human Resources, and Organization Development.

Wade is actively engaged in coaching and consulting with corporate, non-profit, and faith-based organizations. He is a gifted communicator and the creator of the myKUBE™ Seminar & Workshop Series, the Authenticity Equation™, and the Total Engagement Model™. In addition to his professional practice, Wade is an Adjunct Professor at both the undergraduate and graduate levels and currently teaches at Azusa Pacific University, Biola University, and Concordia University. Wade has a Master's Degree in Organizational Leadership and a Doctorate of Psychology in Organizational Management and Change.

Wade's personal mission is to "live and help others live authentic lives where our actions and behaviors (personally, professionally, and organizationally) are in alignment with our values and beliefs." He resides in Orange County,

CA with his daughter Jordan, and their miniature schnau-
zer, Rory.

CHAPTER 1

Understanding RelateAbility

RelateAbility Defined

In short, **RelateAbility is the ability to effectively relate to others.** RelateAbility also includes the potential for transformational relationships with each person we interact with, personally and professionally. In academic terms, we also refer to RelateAbility as "Emotional Intelligence."

Many of our interactions with others seem to be transactional. For example, when going through a drive through, I give you my food order and you give me the food. There is little to no conversation, and often we multitask with our smartphones during the transaction.

What if we chose to look at each interaction with another human being through the lens of RelateAbility?

What if we saw each interaction as a desired connection, where we explore the potential of transformational relationships?

As humans, we are hard-wired for connection. We each desire to feel valued and understood by others. As such, understanding Communication Styles and Core Convictions help us build trust in our relationships with others.

There is no magic spell or miracle pill that can suddenly make our work life perfect. Organizational leadership, strategy, clarity of vision, goal alignment, and the skills each member brings to the team influence and impact individual and team performance. For the purpose of this book, we are focusing on how to improve our ability to build and maintain effective working relationships, which will improve our work-life experiences.

In the workplace, managers empower teams with a deeper understanding of the team members' Communication Styles and Core Convictions. Having regular engagement check-ins help individuals to be more deliberate in their interactions with others. Team productivity is at its best when employees are fully engaged, communicate effectively, and understand each other better.

RelateAbility is a competency or capability that we can develop, grow, and master. By understanding the way we think, feel, and behave, we gain confidence in the greatness of our own being. By understanding the way others think, feel, and behave, we are able to improve our relationships and work together more effectively.

Learning how to best relate with others, RelateAbility provides valuable insights and immediate practical personalized coaching to help managers and their organizations build effective communication and trust among teammates while creating hyper-engaged people.

> RelateAbility is about working together to make work life better.

Realms of RelateAbility

It may seem obvious why we would write a book on RelateAbility and how to improve our relationships in our teams and organization. However, it is important to understand the research behind the choice of using RelateAbility as the focus of our efforts rather than other skills like learning or leadership.

Like the models used for Emotional Intelligence, there are four Realms of RelateAbility:

Self Awareness "What I am experiencing"		Social Awareness "What others are experiencing"
Self-Management "How I choose to behave myself"		Social Management "How I choose to support others"

RelateAbility™

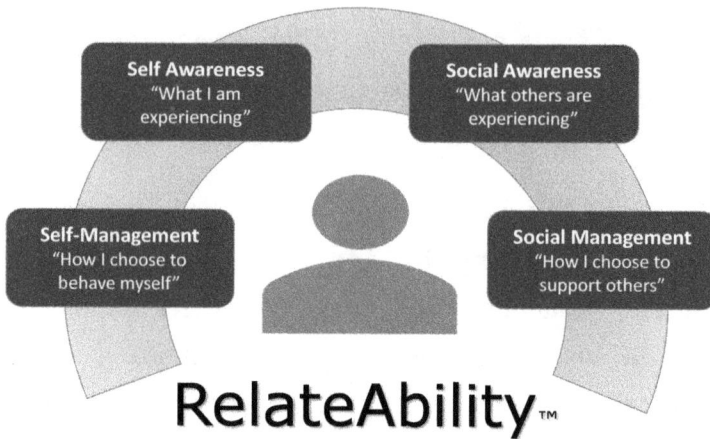

Each realm of RelateAbility is interdependent with the others. As we improve in one realm, we can positively impact our results in the others. In some areas, we will have natural strength and abilities. In others, we have opportunities to grow and develop. All realms are in development throughout our lives, and as we experience more and more relationship situations, we are better able to learn and apply new ways to relate effectively with others.

- **Self-Awareness.** Being aware of your own feelings, thoughts, and behaviors is foundational to the realm of Emotional Intelligence in RelateAbility. By understanding ourselves, we have a better framework to see our strengths as well as our areas of development. In being aware of our responses and how we interact with stress and conflict, we can have the knowledge needed to make better choices on how we respond.

- **Self-Management.** Knowing what we feel and think is very different than effectively managing how we interact with others. We all know people that are very aware of their personality traits, yet choose not to adapt or manage how they are expressing those thoughts and feelings in their personal and professional relationships.

- **Social Awareness.** Like being aware of our own thoughts, feelings, and behaviors, we also can become more purposefully aware of what others are thinking, feeling, and behaving. Too often, we experience life through only our own viewpoint. We fail to consider the viewpoints of others, especially when they are different than our own. Becoming aware of how others are experiencing relationships and teams provides us the knowledge needed to make better choices on how to best manage our response (Self-Management) and how to effectively support them in the given situation.

- **Social Management.** Words like empathy, compassion, understanding, respect, and support are closely tied to Social Management. When we look at our own motives and behaviors (Self-Awareness) and are aware of how others are feeling (Social Awareness), we have the knowledge needed to best manage our responses (Self-Management) and apply the appropriate behaviors that will create the most effective relationships with those around us (Social Management).

Research has shown that by increasing our Emotional Intelligence, or RelateAbility, we are able to positively influence our teams and organizations. In fact, research has shown:

- Individuals with higher RelateAbility have a positive impact on team development, stability, and cohesiveness.

- Teams comprised of emotionally intelligent members have higher team performance, specifically team process effectiveness and team goal focus.

- Having teams develop their emotional intelligence positively impacts team attitudes and directly impacts leader emergence and leadership effectiveness.

RelateAbility and TeamRelate

Throughout the book, we frequently use the terms RelateAbility and TeamRelate. These are not synonymous terms. As defined above, RelateAbility is a competency or skill that can be developed. TeamRelate is the model and tool we are using to build that competency and skill.

For example, a keyboard is a tool that models the "QWERTY" design for key entry. The keyboard is a fantastic invention and has many uses. However, if one does not learn to type, to build the competency or skill using the tool, they will not be as effective as they could be. RelateAbility is like typing, a skill that can be developed. TeamRelate is like the keyboard, a model and tool we can learn to use to make our work lives more effective.

RelateAbility Starts with Self

RelateAbility is often limited to how effectively each person understands themselves. If we do not take the time better understand our own preferences on communication, convictions, and other aspects of our being, it makes it difficult to show understanding, respect, and compassion to others.

RelateAbility starts with a willingness to learn and a desire to grow in our own skills and abilities. This willingness provides us with the opportunity to see ourselves through different "lenses," gaining insight into our natural preferences and how our actions and behaviors impact others we interact with every day.

We must first understand ourselves before we can understand each other. We must first be willing to see ourselves in both our strengths and our areas needing development. We must be honest with ourselves before we can grow in our RelateAbility.

Seeking RelateAbility

There is a proverb that states "What we seek, we will find." At the core of our humanity, we have the choice to look for the good in others, or that of which is lacking. Each of us chooses how we interact with life and with those around us. Seeking RelateAbility is a choice.

In the workplace, RelateAbility is essential for productive teams and organizational effectiveness. As such, we must purposely seek opportunities to connect and build relationships. We need both the "what" and the "how" working together to create productive work teams. It isn't enough to be a good worker and get things done (the "what"). We also need to accomplish our tasks in a way that treats others with respect and understanding (the "how").

We use the following RelateAbility Equation to help frame our discussions:

$$\text{Purposeful Communication} + \text{Purposeful Engagement} = \text{Productive Work Teams}$$

The TeamRelate tool has two components: Communication Styles and Core Convictions. We use the Communication Styles to help make our communication purposeful, and we use the Core Convictions to help make our engagement more purposeful. By understanding the TeamRelate Model, we can better understand ourselves and others, creating more productive work teams.

As you read through this book, ask yourself "Who Am I Being?" Ask whether you are helping or hindering your relationships from achieving their full potential. What we look for, we will find.

CHAPTER 2

Understanding Personality

Personality Defined

Personality is simply described as a pattern of how an individual thinks, feels, and behaves.

We know that there are many characteristics that make every person unique. Our patterns of thought, feeling, and behavior are what make us different from each other in meaningful ways.

Science has afforded us to an opportunity to see patterns in how we think, feel, and behave. Research into personality has shown we have predictable behavioral patterns that can help us better relate with each other.

There is no "Best"

It is important to clearly state that there is no "best" personality. We are all unique and have value and worth in our collective humanity. As we further explore RelateAbility, we must always start from the foundational principle:

> Every personality type is equally important to the effective functioning of our teams and organizations.

Although we might find ourselves more easily relating with individuals that share our same Communication Styles and Core Convictions, it is critical that we never assume that any one personality type is fundamentally better than another.

Nature and Nurture

There is a long-standing debate on whether aspects of our personality are born in us or are the result of our life experiences. There are those that believe behavior is largely inherited and focus on the relationship between our biology and behavior, referred to as Nature. There are those that believe behavior is largely shaped by our environment and life experiences, referred to as Nurture.

The developers of TeamRelate believe that our personality is shaped by both Nature and Nurture. This approach allows us to look at the complexity of human personality in a continuum. Personality is a combination of natural or predetermined traits and aspects that are learned and developed.

As such, we have components of our personality that we cannot change, and many other components that can be developed. RelateAbility is an ability that honors our natural styles and also provides us the freedom to adapt and grow with our environment.

Background and Research History

RelateAbility is anchored in the scientific research of personality and the historical experience of human interaction. The study of personality has a broad and complex history. Provided below are highlights of key personality research that has informed the TeamRelate Model.

2200 B.C.—A Focus on Performance

The earliest personality testing dates back over 4000 years, beginning with the Chinese around 2200 B.C. Testing focused on how individuals performed on certain tests, like penmanship, for example. The purpose of the tests was to determine who would be chosen for civil service positions in Peking.

300 B.C.—A Focus on the Physical

Around 300 B.C., the Greek philosopher Aristotle wrote a short paper on how to distinguish an individual's personality based upon their physical characteristics. He argued that examining a person's hair, forehead, eyebrows, lips, and other bodily features could determine several personality characteristics, such as how wise, foolish, healthy, or deceitful a person was.

1900's

1921: Carl Jung, noted Swiss psychoanalyst and psychiatrist, wrote his theory of personality in a book entitled *Psychological Types.* Dr. Jung introduced the concept of Personality Types, stating that people have different preferences for how they function. He invented the "functional types" or "psychological types" of Introversion and Extroversion. The first serious, validated scientific assessments began during World War I. They were used to screen out army recruits who might be susceptible to shell shock.

1928: William Marston published *Emotions of Normal People,* which introduced the DISC Theory. Marston viewed people behaving along two dimensions, with their attention being either passive or active, depending on the individual's perception of his or her environment as favorable or antagonistic. He placed the axis at right angles, four quadrants form. Each quadrant describes a behavioral pattern: (D) Dominance, (I) Inducement, (S) Submission, and (C) Compliance. The system came to prominence as part of the US Army's recruitment process during the years preceding WWII, and then became a popular tool in the commercial sector.

1943: Over a period of forty years, Isabel Briggs Myers and her mother, Katharine Cook Briggs, created the Myers-Briggs Type Indicator (MBTI). MBTI is based on the ideas of Carl Jung. Motivated by her observation of the waste of human potential during WWII, in 1943, Myers further developed these ideas into a system to provide an easy way for everyone to understand and appreciate the Jungian personality types.

1949: Donald Snygg and Arthur W. Combs introduced a theory of personality called the Phenomenal Field Theory. This theory stated that all behavior is influenced by the conscious mind and can be understood if the researcher sees the world through the individual's eyes and mind. Similar to the saying, "You can't understand a person until you have walked a mile in their shoes," we can choose to consider what another person is thinking and experiencing to better understand and relate with them.

1953: Carl Rogers created 19 Propositions as a foundation for studying personality. The propositions were principles rather than stages of types. His primary focus was on the development of the self-concept and how people develop and grow in their understanding of themselves and others. These Propositions create a set of assumptions and guidelines when using personality assessments.

1965: Raymond Bernard Cattell developed a Personality Model that included 16 traits. He described these 16 traits on a continuum. This provides 32 measures and allows for everyone to have some degree of every trait. Cattel is also known for creating a new statistical method of measuring validity called Factor Analysis. This method is still used today as a statistical tool to measure assessments.

1980: Ernest Tupes and Raymond Christal introduced the Big 5 Personality Model, also known as the Five Factor Model (FFM) in 1961. The model became more widely used in the study of personality in the early 1980s. In 1990, J.M. Digman advanced the FFM of personality, which Lewis Goldberg extended to its current form (Extroversion, Agreeableness, Conscientiousness, Neuroticism, and Openness to Experience). These Five Factors are widely regarded as the gold standard in personality research. The FFM of personality is based on the fundamental principles and goals of Cattell's 16 Personality Factor Model.

1995-Present

1995: University of Southern California professor Michael Williamson saw the need to simplify the many

Personality and Behavioral Models for use in the workplace. By creating a model that focuses on our ability to relate with others, the science becomes practical and more easily applied in the real world of work. He created Communication Styles and Core Convictions that are the foundation to the TeamRelate Model. In 2003, he created the 24 questions that are used in the TeamRelate Survey. The remainder of this book details the TeamRelate Model and how it can be used to increase RelateAbility.

2007: Dr. Michael Williamson partnered with Dr. Mark Vickers to launch WorkTraits 1.0, the system that measures Communication Style and consulted with hundreds of organizations and teams to increase their effectiveness. Dr. Vickers created detailed profiles, coaching and mentoring insights, and expanded the model to include Checkpoints. Continued research and validation was headed by Dr. Bart Weathington of the University of Tennessee at Chattanooga, a leader in assessing behaviors and values. In 2013, the name "WorkTraits" was changed to "TeamRelate."

2015: Ceridian acquired TeamRelate to further enhance their Human Capital Management (HCM) System. Ted Malley, Chief Customer Officer, lead the integration of the TeamRelate model into Ceridian's Dayforce HCM technology. As a result, 3000 customers currently using Dayforce have access to the fully integrated TeamRelate assessment, profiles, coaching, and mentoring insights to use in their Talent Management processes. Dr. Brian O'Leary and Dr. Kate Rogers of the University of Tennessee at Chattanooga continue to provide research and validation testing on the TeamRelate Model and Technology.

2016: Dr. Wade McNair, an Organizational Psychologist and Human Capital Strategist, joined the TeamRelate team to further the strategy and research around TeamRelate and enhance the model for building workplace relationships and organizational engagement. His contributions to the TeamRelate Model include additional research to support the model and the application of RelateAbility to Emotional Intelligence, Workforce Engagement, Conflict, Trust, and Improving RelateAbility. Wade is the co-author of *RelateAbility: Working Together to Make Work Life Better* in partnership with Ceridian's Chief Customer Officer, Ted Malley.

CHAPTER 3

Understanding TeamRelate Communication Styles

The purpose of this book is to help us understand ourselves and others in order to increase our RelateAbility. In the workplace, communication is critical to working together, so the logical place to start is with our Communication Styles.

Focus and Function

To better understand ourselves and others, we will be concentrating our view on two aspects of personality that have a high impact on our RelateAbility. These aspects are Focus and Function.

Focus: Task and Relationship

Each person has a preference for how they get work done. We refer to this aspect of personality as our "Focus." Some people focus primarily on achieving work through tasks, while others focus primarily on achieving work through relationships.

People with a Task Focus place a high value on reaching goals and objectives on schedule. They tend to prioritize accomplishing tasks over maintaining relationships and focus on what people achieve more than who they know.

People with a Relationship Focus view the time taken to build relationships as key to achieving good results. They tend to prioritize maintaining relationships over accomplishing tasks on time and focus more on who they know than on what they themselves can achieve.

As stated earlier about personality, there is no "best" focus. We need people of both Task Focus and Relationship Focus working together to accomplish goals as a team.

Function: Internal and External

Each person has a preference for how they interact with their environment. We refer to this aspect of personality as "Function." Some prefer to function more externally, while others prefer to function internally. There is no "best" function and people with both internal and external functions are needed to effectively achieve team goals.

People with an external function prefer working in larger groups, enjoy leading teams, prefer to interact with many people when making decisions, and recharge their energy when working with others.

People with an internal function prefer working with smaller groups, enjoy leading "behind the curtain," prefer to interact with a select few when making decisions, and recharge their energy spending time alone.

The TeamRelate Communication Styles: DEFT

The four TeamRelate Communication Styles are based upon the dimensions of focus and function that we just discussed.

Communication Style is a description of an individual's natural preference of focus and function. Every individual has components of all Communication Styles, but it is the strongest or most natural style that dominates the rest.

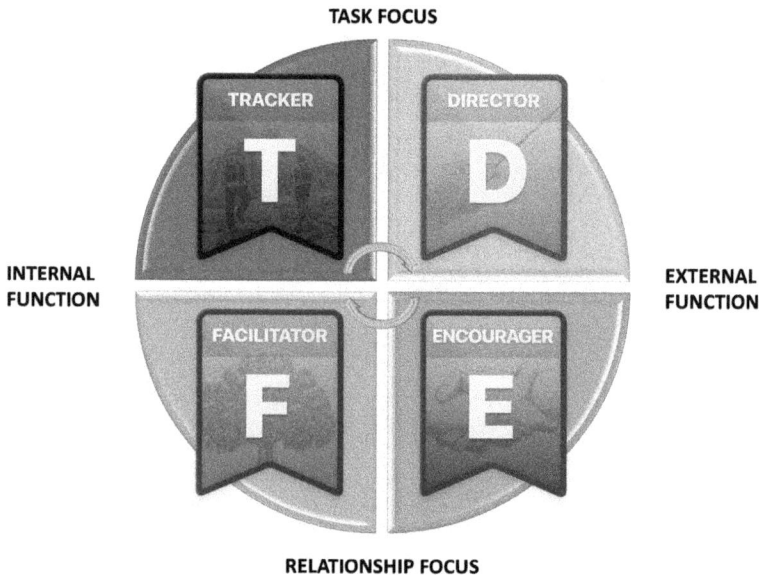

For quick reference, below is a summary of the four Communication Styles:

Director (D): The Director style refers to the degree to which an individual needs to be in charge or in control. They are highly task-focused and prefer to interact with and lead others.

Encourager (E): The Encourager style refers to the degree to which someone is externally and socially oriented. They are highly relationship-focused and prefer to interact with and influence others.

Facilitator (F): The Facilitator style refers to the degree to which an individual is purposeful and patient. They are highly relationship-focused and prefer to work in small groups or collaborate behind the scenes.

Tracker (T): The Tracker style refers to the degree to which an individual is careful about "tracking down" and taking care of details. They are highly task-focused and prefer to work in small groups and lead processes.

For each Communication Style, we will provide an overview of the style, what motivates each style, general characteristics, strengths, and blind spots. We will also provide short examples of how each Communication Style may communicate in the workplace.

Style 1 – Director

This Communication Style refers to people that have a personality preference for Task Focus and External Function.

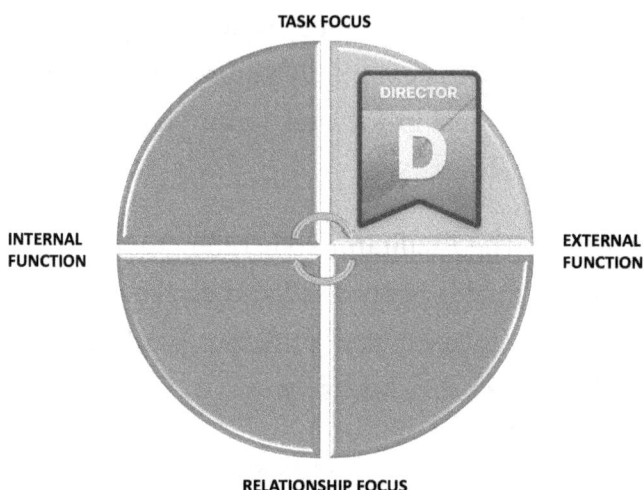

The Director style refers to the degree to which an individual needs to be in charge or in control. It is commonly known as the "Performance" trait, as Directors seek to lead team and organizational performance.

Individuals whose highest score is for the "D" trait need to be in charge and in control. They are strong-willed, and they expect their ideas and decisions to prevail and to be respected.

- **What they say:** Only what is seen as relevant, brief, and bottom line.

- **What they hear**: Sometimes only what they want, and will tune out if too much detail is given.

- **What they need**: For you to get to the point, be factual, and less emotional.

General Behaviors
- Likes to make final decisions
- Needs to be in charge
- Authoritative
- Decides on facts not impulses, analytical
- Acts on environment
- Strong-willed
- Needs the bottom line, to the point
- Gives orders
- Sees the "big picture"
- Commands respect

Strengths
- Decisive
- Good in crisis
- Natural leader
- Proactive
- Visionary

Blind Spots
- Stubborn
- Poor listener
- Difficult to let others lead
- Easily dissatisfied with current situation

- Can gloss over details

<u>Example:</u>

During Erin's meeting with a co-worker, Erin repeats, "Does that make sense?" after explaining an assignment. This "clarifying" remark might seem abrasive to those with differing traits, however Erin's intent is not to be rude. She is direct and likes to get to the point.

Style 2 – Encourager

This Communication Style refers to people that have a personality preference for Relationship Focus and External Function.

The Encourager trait refers to the degree to which someone is externally and socially oriented. It is commonly known as the "People" trait, as Encouragers seek to encourage team and organizational relationships.

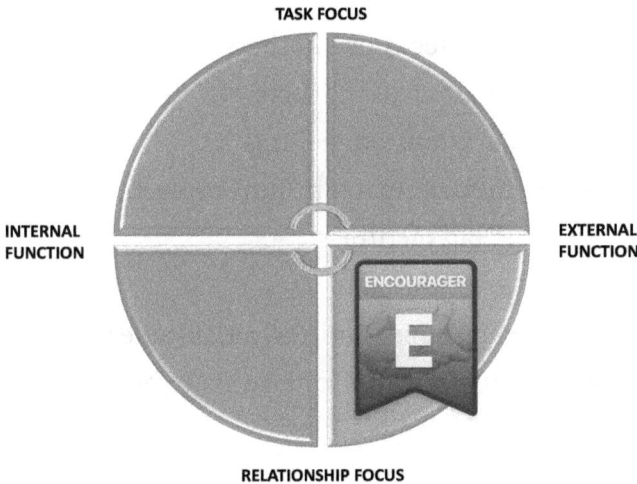

Encouragers are highly sociable, people-oriented, outgoing individuals, who are good communicators with a persuasive Communication Style. They are good at encouraging and motivating others.

- **What they say:** They say a lot, often exaggerate to make a point, and speak with emotion.

- **What they hear:** Broad strokes of conversations, often missing details. They tend to interrupt.

- **What they need:** They need you to let them talk and share their emotional enthusiasm.

General Behaviors
- Likes to encourage, motivate people
- Makes friends easily, extroverted
- Talkative
- Not easily discouraged
- Sensitive to feelings of others
- Acts without all of the facts
- Makes decisions on feelings
- Wants to participate in "fun" projects
- Sees the "big picture"
- Acts on environment
- Inspired by opportunities, a risk-taker
- Needs early rewards, or else changes course

Strengths
- Brings energy to team
- Engaging
- Optimistic
- Enthusiastic
- Can "sell" ideas

Blind Spots
- Overly talkative
- Impractical

- Easily distracted
- Exaggerates stories/facts
- Frustrated by bureaucracy

Example:

When Ashley gets to work on Monday, she is still floating on air from her weekend. She can't help smiling and laughing to all her co-workers who will pay attention to her stories about her weekend adventures.

Style 3 – Facilitator

This Communication Style refers to people that have a personality preference for Relationship Focus and Internal Function.

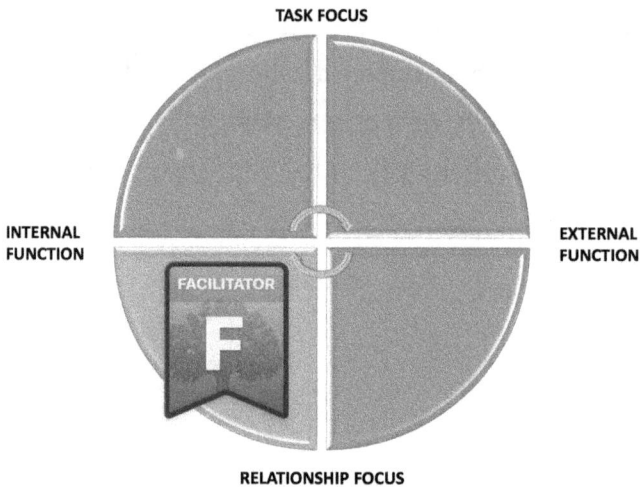

The Facilitator trait refers to the degree to which an individual is collaborative and patient. It is commonly known as the "Productivity" trait, as Facilitators seek to facilitate team and organizational collaboration.

Facilitators tend to be a calming force who prefer supportive roles. They are nice people to have around because they seek understanding in situations and work hard to gain approval. Facilitators pride themselves on being part of the Team, as well as their role in facilitating team effectiveness.

- **What they say:** They don't say much and tend to be reserved and speak in friendly, gentle tones, often asking questions for better understanding.

- **What they hear:** Everything. When others won't listen, Facilitators will.

- **What they need:** They need to be appreciated for listening.

General Behaviors
- May defer to strong leadership
- Seeks approval, eager to please
- Able to wait
- Sets own pace, steady
- Warm, gentle, kind
- Reserved, quiet, often soft-spoken
- Avoids conflict
- Seeks understanding and clarity
- Prefers high productivity over perfection
- Prefers daily routine, even repetitive tasks
- Responds to environment, reactive

Strengths
- Patient
- Supportive
- Reliable
- Can easily gauge mood of team
- Private

<u>Blind Spots</u>
- Indecisive
- Follower
- Slow-paced
- Hard to see the "big picture"
- Slow to speak up

<u>Example:</u>

Mark has a gentle, calming tone. When asking for something in an email, he frequently uses phrases such as "I hate to bother you" or "if you wouldn't mind." He hates to interrupt or express a sense of urgency. Likewise, he does not appreciate when someone demands a project from him without due notice.

Style 4 – Tracker

This Communication Style refers to people that have a preference for Task Focus and Relationship Function.

The Tracker trait refers to the degree to which an individual is careful about "tracking down" and taking care of details. It is commonly known as the "Process" trait, as Trackers seek to maximize effectiveness through detailed data and effective team and organizational processes.

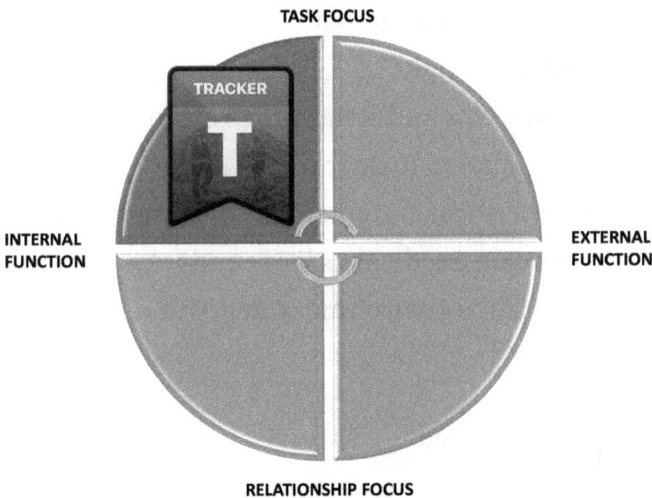

They prefer to follow-up and carry out assignments given to them by authorities they respect rather than to initiate action steps conceived on their own.

- **What they say**: Everything in detail. They give you the whole story.

- **What they hear**: Everything, but want more. Need detail or can feel misled.

- **What they need**: More than anything, they need to be understood. Listen to them, and ask for clarity.

General Behaviors
- Keeps track of details
- Neat, orderly, highly-organized
- Needs clear instructions
- Respects authority, policy, the law
- Keeps the rules, goes by the book
- Seeks the truth, factual
- Needs to be right
- Uses systems and structure to ensure accuracy
- Prefers quality to quantity
- Can be critical, judgmental, concerned with reality
- Needs closure, dislikes loose ends
- Responds to environment, reactive

Strengths
- Detail-oriented
- Systematic
- Cautious
- Tenacious in accuracy
- Ability to see red flags

Blind Spots
- Hard to see the "big picture"
- Slow to think outside of the box

- Slow to change
- Inflexible
- Not a risk-taker

<u>Example:</u>

At home, Kaitlin cannot fall asleep without clearing her mind of all the tasks that she wants to complete tomorrow. She may get up from bed to write them down so she won't forget. At work, Kaitlin likes to make a list of daily duties. She enjoys crossing them off after each is completed. The act of crossing it off gives her a sense of accomplishment.

CHAPTER 4

Understanding Personal Values

Having reviewed our Communication Styles, we now look at another critical component to help increase our RelateAbility: our Personal Values. In the TeamRelate model, we refer to them as Core Convictions.

The Nature of Values

There are six principles that form the foundation of Values Theory. These six principles guide us in our understanding of the nature of Values.

Values are directly linked to our emotions

Values are a set of beliefs that resonate with who we are. As such, there is a direct link from our values to our emotions. When we feel our values are not being appreciated, we feel disrespected. When we feel our values are being honored, we feel supported and validated. The intensity that we exhibit emotions is related to the priority and importance of the values being discussed. Although all values are directly linked to our emotions, each person will display those emotions differently.

Values drive our choices and actions

As a set of beliefs, our values drive our choices and actions. We take action on what we care about most. As we look at our behaviors, we can see what we value. For example, we would expect that a person valuing education would choose to spend their time, money, and energy on actions that support their ongoing learning, development, and the education of others.

Values are demonstrated over time

Our values, often viewed through our actions and behaviors, are most accurately demonstrated over time. We all have moments when we react to a situation and realize our actions do not necessarily reflect our values. As such, it is important to evaluate behaviors over time to have the most accurate understanding of values.

Values serve as a universal standard to evaluate behavior

We use values as a standard to evaluate both our own and others' behaviors. Values are an integrated part of being human, and it is in our nature to use them to select, evaluate, and understand the world around us, events that are occurring, and our relationships with others. Values are also used to understand individual, team, and organizational culture. They act as guidelines for developing strategy, identifying priorities, and operational decision making.

Values are unique to each person through importance and priority

Although values are universal in nature, they are unique to each person. Though there may be similarity in values, each of us will place our own importance and priority on values that we identify as our own. This personalization of values often creates conflict when values are shared by individuals or groups but are not seen at the same level of importance or priority.

Values can adjust over time

Unlike personality or Communication Styles, which tend to remain constant over time, values or Core Convictions change over time. Values are demonstrated over time and are also adaptable to the experiences of a person over time. Value development has a significant impact on an organization and an individual's capacity to work within certain environments. The strength of a Core Conviction often grows because this value is either modeled or taught by an individual or organization.

There is no "Ideal"

Similar to Communication Styles, there is no "Ideal" Core Conviction. Of the four, no Core Conviction has greater or lesser value, and every individual will maintain a mix of all four at varying intensities. These Core Convictions have great importance in how we connect, communicate, and effectively work together to make work life better.

However, we will prioritize our Core Convictions and will have at least one that is ranked higher than the others to ourselves. This creates a preference that identifies the primary motivations and value sets for each individual.

Background and Research History

Humanity has been discussing values for centuries. More recently, research has been conducted to identify what values form the basis of our behaviors and which values are universal in nature. Let's review a short history of Values Research.

1951 - Values in Sociology

Parsons and Shils emphasized that values, in relation to sociology, are believed to help ease the conflict between individual and collective interests. Values serve as an important function by enabling individuals to work together to realize desirable goals collectively.

1961 - Values in Anthropology

Classic conception of values in anthropology got its start by Florence Kluckhohn and Fred Strodtbeck, anthropologists with the Harvard Values Project. From this perspective, values are what answer our basic existential questions to help provide meaning in people's lives. They identified four basic questions that reveal differing cultural orientations to Time, Natural Environment, Relating to Other People, and Motive for Behaving in Different Societies. Anthropologists now had their Values Orientation Theory and the processes to measure cultural orientations in different societies.

1973 - The Rokeach Tradition

One of the biggest contributors to values research was Milton Rokeach, a Polish-American Social Psychologist. Rokeach's focus on values was dedicated to developing an instrument that measured values which he believed were universal and trans-situational. What he developed is known today as the Rokeach Value Survey (RVS). The Rokeach Value Survey is an instrument made up of 36 value items that are ranked by survey subjects. The items are divided into two sets. The first ones are termed "instrumental values" and refer to values that reflect modes of conduct, such as politeness, honesty, and obedience. The second set refers to "terminal values" that reflect desired end states, such as freedom, equality, peace, and salvation. The RVS has since then been widely used by researchers, as the RVS can be used in a wide range of settings.

1992 - Schwartz Theory of Basic Human Values

One researcher to expand on the RVS was Shalom H. Schwartz, a Social Psychologist and creator of the Theory of Basic Human Values. Schwartz proposed his own model in which there are ten motivational value types that fall along two general dimensions. This model was based on an expanded RVS that was used in 50 countries with more than 44,000 subjects. Schwartz also contributed to the formulation of the Values Scale used to measure values in social learning theory and social cognitive theory.

1990-1995 - Inglehart and Abramson Postmodern Thesis

In a different view of value research, Inglehart's focus was on values and economic development. He theorized how different priorities in values were reflected in different economic changes. He argued that the recent boom of modernization and economic security was due to a shift in values for different counties.

2005 – Systematic Values and Hartman Values Inventory

In 2005, Philosopher Robert S. Hartman introduced the concept of Systematic Values, which he defined as "scripts" that exist in the mind of a person. Ideals, norms, standards, rules, doctrines, and logic systems are all examples of systematic values. Hartman integrated three different types of values (intrinsic, extrinsic, and systematic) to create 18 profile types using the Hartman Value Inventory.

2012 – Schwartz Basic Values Model Refined

Ongoing research by Shalom H. Schwartz established what is now the Basic Values Model. Findings from his research from 82 countries provided further validity that his model is applicable cross-culturally. His research covered diversity of religion, geography, age, gender, and occupational groups. He also created the Portrait of Personal Values, an instrument to measure values for those 11-14 years of age and for individuals in countries that are not educated in Western schools.

CHAPTER 5

Understanding TeamRelate Core Convictions

Core Convictions are the four personal value sets that have significant impact on RelateAbility. They are an expression of attitudes which have a strong bearing on performance and motivation in the workplace. Research has shown that employees' performance and motivation are affected by the collective convictions of the team and organization.

Two Dimensions Creating Four Styles

The set of values determined by research can be grouped into two dimensions.

These dimensions help us better understand Core Convictions by creating four distinct profiles – (A) Ambition, (B) Belief, (C) Compassion, and (D) Discipline.

Dimension 1 – Intrapersonal/Interpersonal

The first dimension for Core Convictions is that of the Interpersonal and Intrapersonal continuum.

Core Convictions that have high Interpersonal preference tend to base their values on the actions that influence and impact their performance and relationships with others. It is a relationship dimension that is external by nature.

Core Convictions that have high Intrapersonal preference tend to base their values on the actions that influence and impact their own performance and relationship with themselves. It is a relationship dimension that is internal by nature.

Dimension 2 – Preservation/Promotion

The second dimension for Core Convictions is that of the Preservation and Promotion continuum.

Core Convictions that have high Preservation preference tend to base their values on a desire for stability and are more hesitant to adapt to change. Often driven by the desire for harmony and peace, those with high Preservation scores focus their energy and efforts on actions that will promote stability, standards, and balance.

Core Convictions that have high Promotion preference tend to base their values on the desire for forward movement and are more likely to be leading and directing change. Often driven by the desire for development and achievement, those with high Promotion preference focus their energy and efforts on actions that will promote growth, development, and attaining new levels of achievement, exploring new ideas, and expanding the ideals they consider of greatest importance.

The TeamRelate Core Convictions: ABCD

The four TeamRelate Core Convictions are based upon the two Dimensions that were discussed earlier: Intrapersonal/Intrapersonal and Preservation/Promotion.

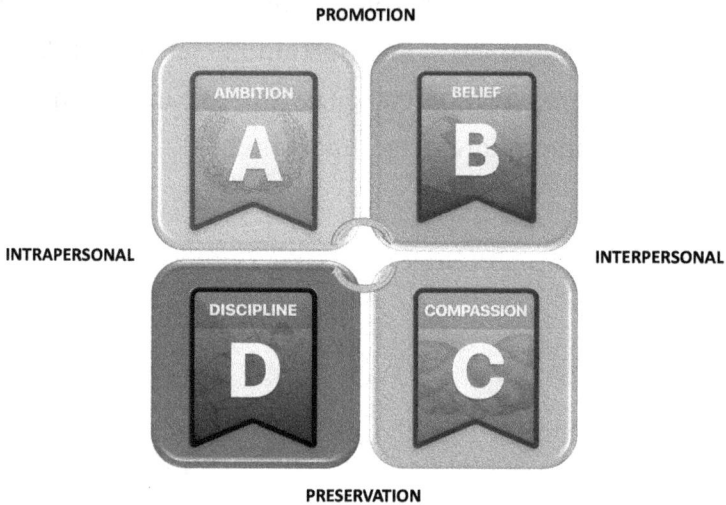

Each individual has their own core values and set of beliefs. To try and create a framework that takes into consideration every value and every belief of every person would be foolish. Instead, TeamRelate looked at four Core Convictions that have the greatest impact on RelateAbility. They are (A) Ambition, (B) Belief, (C) Compassion, and (D) Discipline.

For quick reference, below is a summary of the four Communication Styles:

- **Ambition:** Ambition refers to the degree to which an individual is "forward-looking" and proactive in achieving significant goals.

- **Belief:** Belief refers to the degree to which an individual trusts in and lives according to a predefined ethical system.

- **Compassion:** Compassion refers to the degree to which an individual feels compelled to help those less fortunate.

- **Discipline:** Discipline refers to the degree to which an individual is able to sustain focus and dedication toward the completion of a task or goal.

We will provide an overview of each Core Conviction and its general characteristics. We will also provide a short example of how each Core Conviction may be seen in the workplace.

Conviction A - Ambition

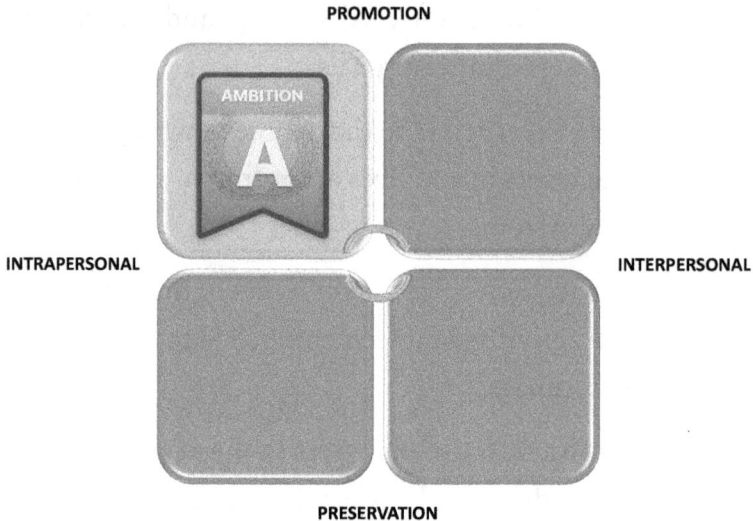

Ambition refers to the degree to which an individual is "forward-looking" and proactive in achieving significant goals.

Individuals whose highest score is for Ambition proactively seek a better future by improving themselves, their organization, or their community. In work settings, they often take the lead and move a team or organization forward.

General Characteristics:
- Forward-looking, can help an organization envision the future
- Optimistic, seeing a better future
- Will take steps to improve self

- Sometimes dismissive of others who don't try to improve themselves
- Self-confident, will often seek leadership roles
- Often willing to assume risk
- Often entrepreneurial, may feel constrained by rigid rules
- Can be seen by others as an overachiever
- Proactive in reaching goals
- Can provide energy to an organization
- Provides initiative for moving projects forward
- Can provide vitality to low performing teams

Example:

Kellie has a fulltime class schedule, works, maintains a relationship, and reads constantly in pursuit of self-improvement. Kellie sets goals for herself regularly, and many of her co-workers wonder where she finds the time for it all.

Conviction B – Belief

Belief refers to the degree to which an individual trusts in and lives according to a predefined ethical system.

Individuals whose highest score is for Belief desire to impact the world through their actions and the promotion of their belief system. They make decisions about behavior based upon their defined views of right and wrong (morality).

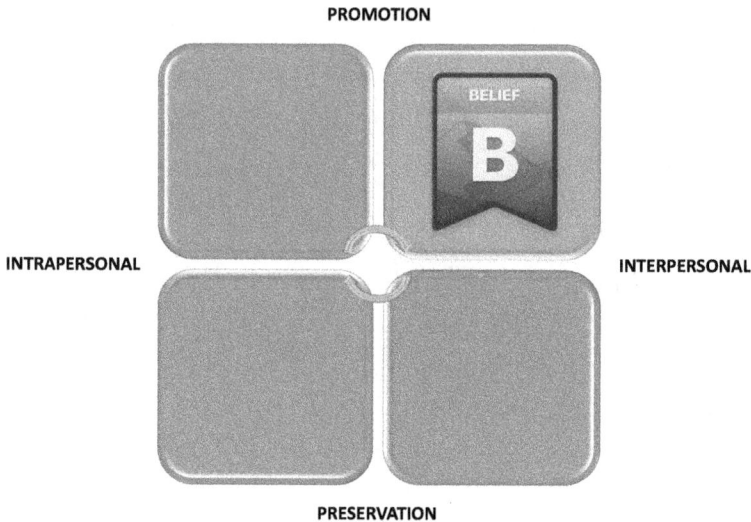

PROMOTION

BELIEF

B

INTRAPERSONAL

INTERPERSONAL

PRESERVATION

General Characteristics

- Often identifies with a set of defined values
- Has a thoughtful but sometimes rigid belief system
- Seeks opportunities to share and converse on values and beliefs
- Has high standards for conduct in the workplace

- Provides a good sounding board for difficult decisions
- Can become good mentors for junior employees
- Will take steps to improve character and support others in theirs
- Needs to see integrity in the management of the organization
- Values honesty, hard work, and personal integrity
- Looks for ways to "live our values" within the organization and align them to the organization's mission, vision, and values

Example:

None of Paden's co-workers could ever remember her using profanity or sarcastic language. Her co-workers knew where Paden stood on issues, and she did her best to live up to her own high standards.

Conviction C - Compassion

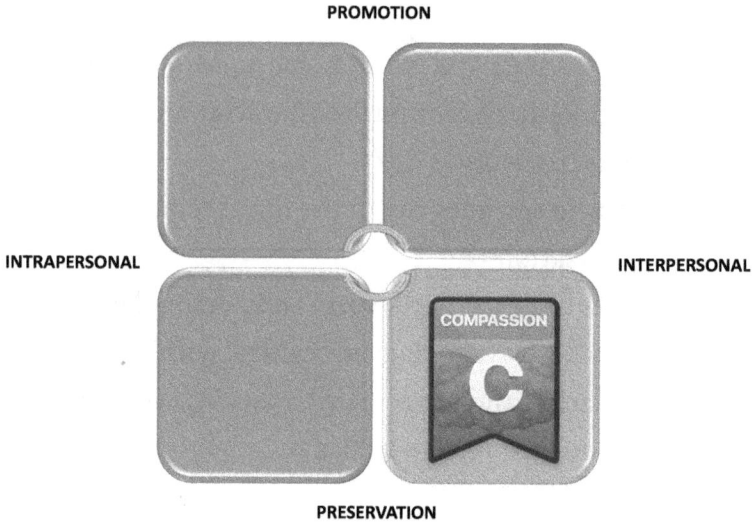

Compassion refers to the degree to which an individual feels compelled to help those less fortunate.

Individuals whose highest score is for Compassion possess a rare quality for giving to others in need. They give their time and resources in order to help others succeed, become self-reliant, or contribute to the well-being of society.

General Characteristics

- Friendly, often good at making people feel welcome
- Hopeful about the human condition and the ability to better oneself
- Can help a team become "client-centered"
- Attracted to careers that are client-centered

- May be seen as too emotional and sometimes irrational in the ways they give
- Others-centered, values long term relationships with employees and clients
- Can help clients feel appreciated
- Often motivated more by the mission than by financial gain
- Values leaders who demonstrate compassion and are giving to others

Example:

Zheila felt the most satisfaction from teaching dance when she could provide it to those who couldn't afford it. She didn't mind that some people viewed her as giving too much of herself in the pursuit of helping others. She believes that helping others is her calling.

Conviction D – Discipline

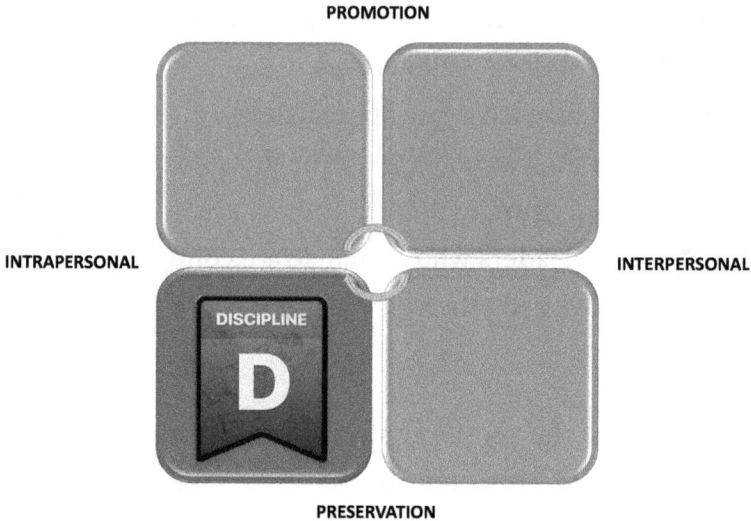

Discipline refers to the degree to which an individual is able to sustain focus and dedication toward the completion of a task or goal.

Individuals whose highest score is for Discipline seek to create stability and effectiveness through the use of standards and processes.

<u>General Characteristics</u>
- Good with "follow-through"
- Can help a team finish projects
- Can make a significant contribution to the goals of a team
- Often displays loyalty to respected leaders and organizations

- May be seen as inflexible, committed to only one way of doing things
- Attracted to organizations with a clear mission and vision
- Passionate about work
- Desires to see timely completion of projects
- Can provide a good example of follow-through for other employees
- Can be good with following up with requests from clients

Example:

Jeff is able to focus on tasks and projects with enthusiasm and determination. He runs for an hour every morning, and even though he may not want to some days, he knows that he dislikes the feeling of breaking his routine. Sometimes Jeff can become too focused on a specific method of achieving a goal, but as a whole, he exemplifies tenacity and hard work.

CHAPTER 6

RelateAbility and Workforce Engagement

Employee Engagement

Employee engagement is a hot topic in many organizations. The Gallup organization has been tracking engagement data for many years, and, unfortunately, the results are not encouraging.

To better understand the research, we must look at the types of Employee Engagement. Most researchers and organizations use a 3-tier definition as shown on the following page. According to the Gallup research, the percentage of U.S. workers that are considered "Engaged" in their jobs has maintained an average of about 30% in the last six years. That is about a third of employees that work with passion and feel connected to their organization.

Engaged	Employees work with passion and feel connected to their organization. They energize and drive the team and company forward.
Not Engaged	Employees just put in their time on the job and are "checked out." They hinder the team and company from moving forward.
Actively Disengaged	Employees are unhappy and actively complain on the job. They undermine and derail the team and company from moving forward.

On average, half (50%) of the employed workforce is considered to be "Not Engaged" in their employment. These employees are often referred to as "checked out" and at work mostly "for the check." "Actively Disengaged" employees, those that are unhappy and actively undermine the success of the team and organization, are averaging just under 20% of the workforce.

> Engaging employees is critical to achieving Organizational Results. Improving RelateAbility of individuals and teams can influence this important measure of organizational success.

Engagement Impact on Organizational Results

Research shows that employee engagement drives organizational effectiveness and growth. Research completed by the Gallup organization accumulated 339 research studies across 230 organizations in 49 industries and 73 countries. The results of their multiple-year analysis of over 1.8 million employees showed a direct correlation between employee/team engagement and organizational outcomes.

The research identified nine organizational areas that are impacted by team engagement. When comparing teams with low engagement to those with high engagement, they found the following impacts in favor of high team engagement:

- 10% increase in customer loyalty
- 21% increase in profitability
- 20% increase in productivity
- 24% reduction in turnover
- 70% reduction in safety incidents
- 28% reduction in shrinkage (theft)
- 41% reduction in absenteeism
- 58% reduction in patient safety incidents
- 40% reduction quality (defects)

Overall, business units in the top half of employee engagement have 78% higher success rate in their own organization and a 113% higher success rate across business units in all the companies that they researched. In other words, teams with higher employee engagement nearly doubled their performance in comparison with those with lower employee engagement.

> Teams that improve and develop their RelateAbility become more engaged and, as a result, have a positive impact on organizational performance.

Managing Change and Team Development

Change Management is a topic that is critically important to Organizational Effectiveness and Workforce Engagement. Increasing RelateAbility in teams will (A) reduce the depth of negative performance and (B) increase time to performance for individuals and teams.

The graphic on the facing page represents what is called the "Change Curve."

When teams experience change, they go through a process called "Storming." This process reduces the Performance and Effectiveness of the team as they seek to resolve issues related to roles, responsibilities, and relationship challenges.

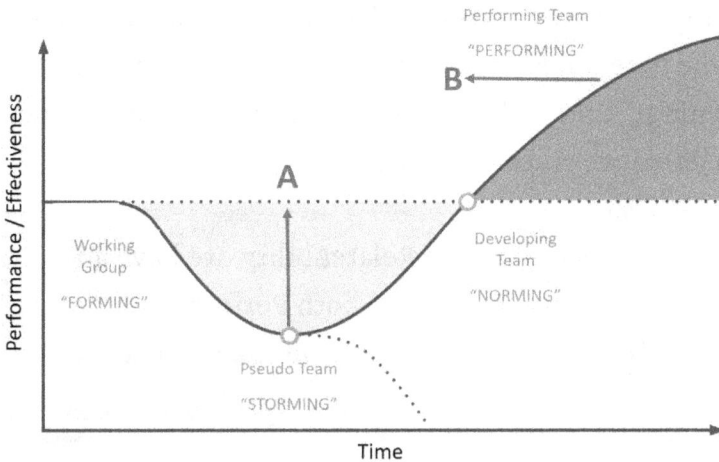

When individuals and teams start with a clear understanding of their own Communication Styles and Core Convictions and how to best use them in their team interactions, we should see a reduction in the depth of the curve relating to this "Storming" stage (noted as "A" on the above graphic). Minimizing length and depth of the storming stage often leads to higher individual engagement and organizational outcomes.

After a team has successfully navigated the "Storming" stage of team development, they enter a phase called "Norming." This stage produces a set of expected performance results and normalizes the way the team works together. If teams choose to continue growth and development, they have the potential to reach beyond the normalized expectations and become "High Performing."

When individuals and teams have training and choose to apply the principles of RelateAbility, we see an increase in the time it takes to move from "Norming" through "Performing," and finally, "High Performing" for the team performance and effectiveness.

> By developing our RelateAbility, we have an opportunity to increase both Performance and Effectiveness at multiple points in a team's development and growth stages.

TeamRelate Engage!

We are committed to furthering the research between RelateAbility, Workplace Engagement, and Organizational Effectiveness. We are currently conducting research to look at how organizations can show improvement and growth in the following areas by focusing on developing RelateAbility with their teams:

- Job Engagement - Physical

- Job Engagement - Emotional
- Job Engagement - Cognitive
- Team Effort
- Team Trust
- Team Cohesiveness
- Team Satisfaction
- Team Conflict – Task and Relationship
- Perceived Organizational Support
- Intent to Stay/Turnover Intentions
- Safety Motivation and Participation

When integrated with ongoing Performance and Development discussions between Managers and their Teams, the use of Communication Styles and Core Convictions as Development tools, people managers are better equipped to improve overall scores of Organizational Engagement.

TeamRelate Communication Styles and Workforce Engagement

Employee engagement data shows the majority of employees are not "Engaged" and that we can improve organizational results by increasing employee engagement.

Understanding how our strengths, how we lead, and where we find motivation in the workplace can give us insight on how Communication Styles can improve engagement.

For each Communication Style, we will provide an overview of how the style interacts with workforce engagement, specifically the strengths they bring to a team, their desired interaction with others, their mindsets about engagement, and their preference for leadership.

Style 1 - Director

Strengths

You need to lead, to manage, and to be in control. You tend to look to the future and plan for it. You set goals and have ideas about how to reach these goals. You tend to be curious about what could be. You have confidence that your ideas will work, and you can be open about the fact that you want those ideas to become the accepted way of doing things.

Interaction

You prefer to keep things moving at a steady to fast pace. In any business matter, you like to get to the bottom line quickly. You may become annoyed with people who speak in generalizations or get onto tangents that are not directly related to the topic. You tend to be all business and rarely engage in frivolous banter.

You are a thinker more than a talker. This is apparent in group situations where you may be quiet and reserved and may need to be drawn into the conversation. Once drawn into the conversation, you are compelled to direct it.

Mindset

You appreciate the approval of others as long as it is sincere. You respect people who are honest, trustworthy, and objective. You have little use for people who try to make good impressions with flattery or who are pretentious or overly impressed with themselves.

Your natural curiosity stays tuned to new, interesting challenges. If the conditions and timing are right, you like to become involved and make things happen.

Leadership

You tend to be assertive, firm, and strong-willed, even forceful or demanding when necessary.

You like to be independent, free to think and act in ways that further your personal goals. You appreciate quality and want things done right. This style may also be reflected in orderliness and in being organized. You want others to take care of details and finish the project, but where things do not meet expected standards, you can become directly involved and hands-on.

You enjoy change, especially opportunities or activities that contribute to outcomes in which you have a vested interest. You tend to put more energy into organizing and initiating projects than in maintaining them once they are underway.

Style 2 - Encourager

Strengths

You are a fast-paced, animated individual, who is very talkative and outgoing. You like to talk to just about anyone, anytime, anywhere.

You tend to talk at a rapid rate and are quite fluent. You frequently use hand gestures to help get your points across. Your volume and variation in verbal expressions also may be distinguishing features.

You are jovial and fun-loving, and you try to keep it on the light side. You relate to people easily and have lots of friends.

You like to be where the action is and usually find a way to be involved in it. You want to be included in the "in-group" wherever one exists, and in these situations, you typically command a good share of the attention.

Interaction

You are naturally enthusiastic, one who likes to encourage and motivate people. At these and other times, you need to be careful not to do all the talking, but to also listen and hear what people have to say. Listening is not a natural habit for you. You need to make a conscious effort to engage people in conversation so that it is not simply a monologue.

You are also diplomatic with an ability to say things that are socially acceptable and not abrasive or offensive. You dislike confrontations and avoid interpersonal conflict as much as possible.

You can be distracted easily, especially if there are opportunities to talk to someone. To stay on track, you need to keep a personal calendar that schedules activities to ensure that projects are finished on time and deadlines are met.

Mindset

You are naturally independent, a person with big ideas, dreams, and goals. You think a lot about the future and what could be, even to the extent of trying to make those dreams become a reality.

You tend to dislike daily chores, routines, or repetitive tasks, and may postpone doing them. To help keep things organized and up-to-date, you need to have access to the latest systems, technology, and/or staff members that follow up and take care of details on your behalf.

Leadership

You prefer to serve in a supportive role rather than being in charge. In the event a leadership role is required, you need to seek counsel from team members, superiors, or other respected authorities.

You can be very persuasive, and that translates into being a natural "seller." If the item is not an actual product, then you sell your opinions, ideas, or points of view. As a salesperson, you have a soft-sell style and may need special training to know when and how to close the deal.

Style 3 - Facilitator

Strengths

You have a style that is warm, gentle, quiet, and reserved. You are friendly, respectful, and considerate of other people.

You are naturally very patient, a trait that may be expressed by behaviors that are steady and dependable, planned and deliberate, not impulsive. You are serious-minded and are not generally inclined to joke around.

You are independent and able to get things done without being micro-managed or constantly told what to do. If the goal is clearly presented and understood, you tend to find ways to reach it, even if every detail about how to get there is not provided.

Interaction

You are a good listener and do so without frequent interruptions or knee-jerk reactions to things that are said, even though you may not agree with every statement.

People with this style tend to be thinkers as opposed to being highly talkative. You do not waste words, may be soft-spoken, and would rarely monopolize the conversation. However, when given the opportunity to facilitate, you are able to be a mediator and positively influence collaboration.

Mindset

You need the security of a daily routine, one without a lot of surprises. You likely are not a visionary with big dreams and goals for the future with well-developed plans for reaching them. You prefer assignments that can be done today and at the end of the day can be checked off the "to do" list.

It may be a challenge for you to keep things orderly and organized. You are neither fussy nor a perfectionist. That may mean that you need help keeping the office or work environment neat and tidy. You have too many other things to do.

You prefer to work in environments that are calm and peaceful, where people get along with each other and there are few disturbances to the daily routine. You prefer plenty of time to complete assignments and dislike deadlines or any task labeled "URGENT!" or "RUSH!"

<u>Leadership</u>

You look to others for strong overall leadership and prefer to take a supportive role. However, you are also capable of solving problems independently and enjoy being trusted to do that.

You prefer quantity to quality. In your case, that probably means high production without perfection. However, your productivity is due to a steady pace rather than a fast, hurried pace.

You are not a risk-taker because risks are potential threats to security. You need to feel secure. That means that you prefer to live with the status quo, unless convinced that changes would not be a threat. You tend to be easygoing and unhurried, with the ability to take most things in stride without feeling the need to change them.

Style 4: Tracker

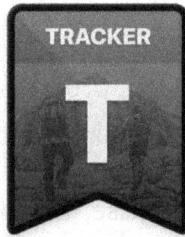

<u>Strengths</u>

You are obsessed with doing things right. That means you rely on, and comply with, rules and regulations, policies and procedures, and respected authorities.

You tend to be a perfectionist, a person who may even be compulsive about being organized and taking care of every detail. For you, everything has a place, and everything must be in its place unless it is being used.

You like to take one step at a time. You probably keep a daily list of things to do and a schedule of events and activities and check them off when they are completed so that there is a sense of progress and clear evidence of accomplishment at the end of the day.

<u>Interaction</u>

You are more of a thinker than one who is outgoing and overly talkative. You choose words carefully so that few are wasted, and they are as accurate and direct and to the point as possible. You frequently back up statements with facts and figures or written documentation from respected authorities.

You are serious-minded, professional, all-business, and are not interested much in joking around.

In areas of your expertise, standards are so high that the work of others typically fails to compare. Thus, your evaluations can often be constructively critical, including suggestions about improvements.

Mindset

You like, and use to great advantage, the latest systems and technologies because they provide valuable tools for managing information and maintaining order.

You want to be right, hate to be wrong, and hate to be embarrassed. Sometimes you may not take action for fear of being wrong or for fear that asking for help might lead to embarrassment. Those situations can be very stressful for you.

You are conscientious, a person who follows up well, puts on the finishing touches, completes the task, and gets closure. Those attributes make you a highly valuable team player.

You choose friends carefully and undoubtedly prefer those with common standards and similar mindsets and approaches. You would be uncomfortable around people with poor taste or those whose personal space is untidy and disorganized.

Leadership

You look to others for leadership, preferring to support respected leadership rather than to be solely in charge. You are very responsible when it comes to carrying out work assignments, as long as the goal is clearly defined and the instructions are thorough and fully understood.

You are highly focused on the immediate tasks at hand, the things that need to be done right now or today.

You are extremely quality-oriented. While productivity is important, the quality of performance is more important. In fact, productivity undoubtedly is reduced because you put in so much time getting every detail done perfectly.

TeamRelate Core Convictions and Workforce Engagement

As opposed to Communication Styles, Core Convictions change over time, and their development has a significant impact on an organization and an individual's capacity to work within certain environments.

Clearly all four Core Convictions are important and are likely convictions you want to see in your work environment. The presence or absence of these convictions at work will affect your attitude and job satisfaction. In fact, research has shown that employees with similar convictions to their co-workers and company are more likely to be:

- Satisfied with their job
- Committed to their organization
- Reluctant to leave their company

Therefore, part of your "fit" with a company involves the degree of harmony between your convictions and those of your company. General company Core Convictions are often referred to as things like Vision, Mission, and Values. In any case, it is important to recognize how your convictions shape your attitude toward work and your work environment.

For each Core Conviction, we will provide insight as to the preferred working environments and recommendations on how you can best perform in your organization.

Conviction A: Ambition

If Ambition is your strongest conviction, you are proactive in reaching goals—an achiever. Your conviction of Ambition provides an organization with energy to complete projects and inspire teams.

AMBITION A	Preferred Environment	To Best Perform
	Respect for hard work	Work on projects that have lasting organizational value
	Clear mission and vision	Learn from senior management
	Opportunities for promotion	Develop inter-personal and professional skills
	Education and development	Become more than a visionary
	Challenging traditional paradigms	Execute plans that build your company

Conviction B: Belief

If Belief is your strongest conviction, you value integrity, fairness, and moral excellence. Your conviction of Belief can provide an ethical perspective when difficult decisions need to be made.

BELIEF B	Preferred Environment	To Best Perform
	Honesty, hard work, and fairness	Look for opportunities to mentor junior employees
	Leaders who live exemplary lives	Lead by example
	Recognition for integrity	Work on projects that promote personal growth
	Education and professional development	Realize your ethical system is more clearly defined than most people's
	Conscientiousness about quality in customer service	Seek to live out your values

Conviction C: Compassion

If Compassion is your strongest conviction, you possess a rare quality for giving to others in need. Your conviction of Compassion provides an organization with a client-centered perspective.

COMPASSION C	Preferred Environment	To Best Perform
	Long-term relationships with employees and clients	Are inspired by the mission and vision of your organization
	Helping employees and clients succeed	Build long-term relationships with staff and clients
	Leaders who give to the community	Have realistic expectations about whom you are able to help
	Programs that promote care for others	Work on projects that promote personal or societal well-being
	An individual's ability to better society	Are able to see tangible ways your work affects others

Conviction D: Discipline

If Discipline is your strongest conviction, you have the ability to sustain your focus and dedicate yourself to the completion of a task or goal. Your conviction of Discipline provides an organization with tenacity, helping them "stay the course" and never lose sight of their mission and vision.

DISCIPLINE D	Preferred Environment	To Best Perform
	Precision, discipline, and timely completion of projects	Work on projects that require precision and execution
	Clear mission and vision	Are passionate about the goals of the company
	Integrity in their processes	Model "follow-through" to junior employees
	New challenges to solve	Help teams finish projects and show impact
	Opportunities to create impact	Maintain timely follow-up with client requests

CHAPTER 7

RelateAbility and Workplace Conflict

Understanding Workplace Conflict

Conflict in the workplace is expected. Whenever we have people interacting with other people, conflict is a real possibility. The goal is not to eliminate conflict from the workplace, but rather to understand it and seek ways to effectively resolve it.

There are 3 types of Workplace Conflict:

- **Goal Conflict** – conflict that arises when individuals do not agree on the actions needed to reach a goal, or disagree on the goal itself.

- **Values Conflict** – conflict that arises from perceived or incompatible values or beliefs, often impacted by cultural, political, and religious differences.

- **Relational Conflict** – conflict that arises when individual styles and ways of working are perceived to be negative or unwanted, often called Personal Conflict.

Impact of Workplace Conflict

When individuals have conflict, it impacts the team and the organization. If the conflict remains unresolved, the impact is negative. If the conflict is effectively resolved, the impact can be more positive. Understanding how our Communication Styles and Core Convictions interact with Values Conflict and Relational Conflict is an important step to improving our RelateAbility in both our personal and our professional lives.

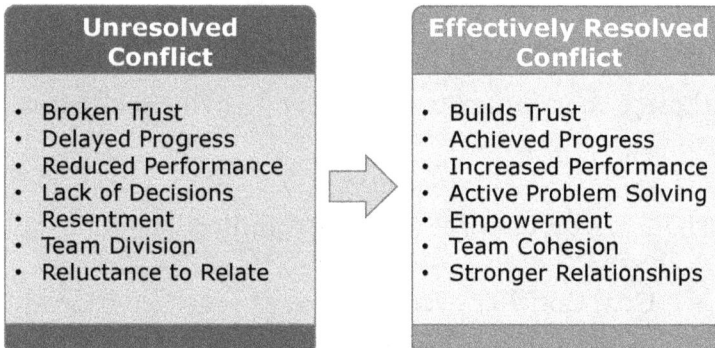

Unresolved Conflict	Effectively Resolved Conflict
• Broken Trust • Delayed Progress • Reduced Performance • Lack of Decisions • Resentment • Team Division • Reluctance to Relate	• Builds Trust • Achieved Progress • Increased Performance • Active Problem Solving • Empowerment • Team Cohesion • Stronger Relationships

Finding Common Ground

In the workplace, we often experience Values Conflict. A value conflict is created between individuals who have differences in their long-held beliefs and worldviews. Value conflict can also be the result of social, cultural, political, or religious differences. As a result, value conflict is not resolved easily because the conflict is not necessarily fact-based.

In fact-based conflict, individuals can be persuaded to change their viewpoints. For value conflicts, logic and constructed arguments are not effective in changing a person's Core Conviction. Whether we are dealing with value conflict on an individual basis, with teams, or between organizations or even countries, the traditional methods of conflict resolution are only effective once we can find common ground.

Finding common ground is a commitment to determining a value or outcome that is held at high priority for both parties involved. For example, a team may consist of members with value conflict. The common ground for these individuals may be a shared desire for the team to be successful in achieving the team goals. By starting from a place of shared interest, value conflicts can be reframed into an agreement to reach a common goal.

Finding common ground does not mean finding absolute agreement. Instead, it is the foundation to building trust and establishing a shared goal that both individuals can use as the building blocks to reach further agreement.

Communication Style Conflict

One of the key contributors to Relational Conflict is how we communicate and interact with others. Team relationships are often put in conflict when a natural characteristic or Communication Style of a team member is perceived as being negative or unwanted.

It has been said that "me just being me can cause conflict with you just being you." Our natural Communication Style can be perceived and experienced by others as negative and even offensive. Therefore, it is important that we understand how our natural styles can be seen by others, especially if they are being misapplied or overused in a specific situation or team context.

Also, we must understand that, even in the best use of our Communication Styles, there will be those who are more sensitive to certain characteristics. This can be based on previous negative experiences with someone sharing your Communication Style, assumptions and beliefs of cultural norms, or personal preferences for Communication Styles like their own.

Below are some examples of how each of the Communication Styles could be perceived in negative ways. Please note that the perceptions are not tied to a motivation or desire by the individual, but rather how others view or experience the characteristics listed.

Style 1 - Director

DIRECTOR D	Characteristics	May Be Perceived As...
	Competitive	Wanting to win at all costs
	Assertive	Impulsive and disrespectful of others
	Innovative	Taking unnecessary risk
	Decisive	Always needing to be in charge
	Independent	Unfriendly and dismissive of others
	Achievement	Focused only on self promotion and power

Style 2 - Encourager

ENCOURAGER E	Characteristics	May Be Perceived As...
	Inspiring	Unrealistic and lacking substance
	Charming	Superficial and fake
	Trusting	Naïve and easily influenced
	Talkative	Insecure and poor listener
	Expressive	Needing attention and validation
	Spontaneous	Lacking focus and follow through

Style 3 - Facilitator

FACILITATOR F	Characteristics	May Be Perceived As...
	Reliable	Unable to say no or challenge ideas
	Systematic	Stuck in their own process
	Loyal	Unable to see from other points of view
	Energetic	Overwhelming and threatening
	Supportive	Unable to make tough decisions
	Generous	Easily taken advantage of

Style 4 - Tracker

TRACKER T	Characteristics	May Be Perceived As...
	Analytical	Heartless and uncaring
	Detailed	Lost in weeds, unable to see big picture
	Cautious	Resistant to change and growth
	Precise	Fussy and perfectionist
	Thoughtful	Timid or lacking confidence
	Disciplined	Rigid and uncreative

To better understand how these characteristics can be perceived to be negative, we need to better understand how our natural characteristics can be seen as negative.

There are three ways that we can evaluate our own characteristics. They also provide a framework for opening discussion with those with whom we have relational conflict. They are:

- **Frequency** – How often the characteristic is displayed. Imagine a child in a car constantly asking "Are we there yet?" It is not the question that is causing the conflict, it's the repeated use of the question, or Frequency of the behavior that is creating a challenge.

- **Intensity** – The amount of energy behind the characteristic being displayed. Passion is great, but can be intense for others to handle sometimes. When we "come on strong," we often "put others off." The Intensity of the passion behind our behaviors can cause conflict, while the behavior itself may not be the issue.

- **Context** – The situation in which the characteristic is being displayed. Research has shown that laughing is a good thing. It promotes well-being, builds relationship, and has positive impact on others. However, laughing at a funeral may be seen as offensive. Conflict can be created when our behaviors are used in a context that is seen by others as inappropriate.

When we find ourselves in Relational Conflict with others, it may be the result of our natural behaviors being perceived in a negative way. It is in these moments that we can seek understanding, choose positive intent, control our "volume," and respond rationally.

CHAPTER 8

Improving Your RelateAbility

Seek Understanding

We all have a need to be understood, to be listened to, and to feel heard. When communicating with other styles, it is most helpful to know what each style needs to feel connected and validated.

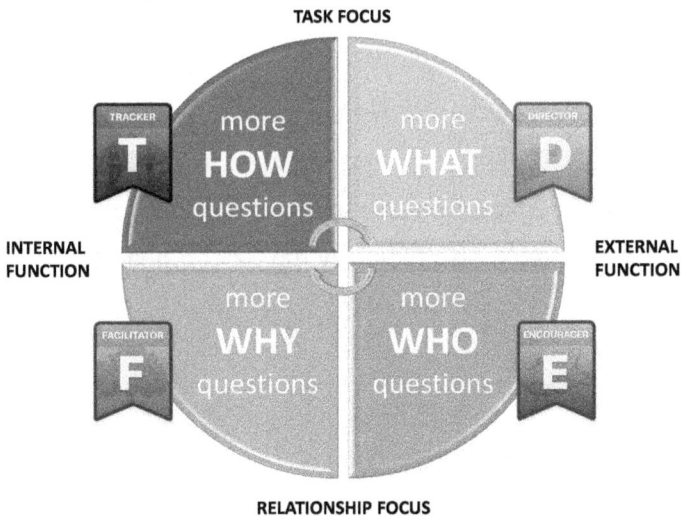

Here is how each Communication Style seeks to be understood:

- **Directors** want to discuss how a project/action will impact PERFORMANCE. Asking a Director more "WHAT" questions will allow them to express their natural preference and feel they have been heard and understood.

- **Encouragers** want to discuss how a project/action will impact PEOPLE. Asking encourages more "WHO" questions will allow them to express their natural preference and feel they have been heard and understood.

- **Facilitators** want to discuss how a project will impact PRODUCTIVITY. Asking facilitators more "WHY" questions will allow them to express their natural preference and feel they have been heard and understood.

- **Trackers** want to discuss how a project will impact PROCESSES. Asking trackers more "HOW" questions will allow them to express their natural preference and feel they have been heard and understood.

Positive Intent

It is vitally important that we not assume negative intent in our relationships with others. This includes when others may misperceive our behaviors as negative and when we perceive others with characteristics that rub us the wrong way.

One of the best ways to respond to Conflict is to "choose curiosity." By placing ourselves in a place of asking questions and seeking to understand others, we move from a place of defensiveness to a place of understanding.

Choosing to say "I wonder..." instead of "They are..." removes the opposition mindset and creates the space for learning and growing in our RelateAbility. Positive intent allows us to reframe the situation from one that needs to be defended to one that needs to be solved together.

We make choices every day to either effectively resolve conflicts and improve our RelateAbility or allow ourselves to be hindered and hurt by conflict left unresolved. Ultimately, it is our choice.

"Volume" Control

Imagine you are driving in the car listening to your favorite music at the volume level you enjoy. You pick up your grandma and the first thing she says to you is, "Turn that down." How do you respond? In this situation, you have a few options:

- Tell grandma that it's your car and the music will stay exactly as it is.

- Turn the music even higher to show you are in control.

- Turn off the music in exasperation.

- Adjust the volume to a level that you both can enjoy.

If the goal is to have a good relationship with grandma, it would be best to adjust the volume to a level you both can enjoy. Doing the other three options will hinder or hurt your relationship with grandma, and that is not seeking RelateAbility.

This principle applies when we are communicating with others in the workplace. Our ultimate goal is to have healthy and happy work relationships, yet we often forget this goal when we are having relational conflict.

Choosing to adjust our volume, or to communicate in a way that others will best receive, is not diminishing our own uniqueness, desires, and natural styles. We are not asking ourselves to change; we are instead asking ourselves to adapt to the situation to build and better RelateAbility.

Respond Rationally

In relational and values conflict, we often find ourselves in a state of heightened emotions. Many would agree that we don't make our best decisions when we are emotional. In fact, some of our worst decisions are the result of not taking the time to Pause, THINK, and Respond Rationally.

Vicktor Frankl was a psychologist that survived inside the Nazi concentration camps during WWII. He was able to use his time as a captive to better understand the nature of people experiencing internal and external conflict. One of his most profound quotes speaks to the space between the action we experience and our choice as to how we will respond. He said:

> We who lived in concentration camps can remember the men who walked through the huts comforting others, giving away their last piece of bread. They may have been few in number, but they offer sufficient proof that everything can be taken from a man but one thing: the last of the human freedoms—to choose one's attitude in any given set of circumstances, to choose one's own way. Between stimulus and response, there is a space. In that space is our power to choose our response. In our response lies our growth and our freedom. — Vicktor Frankl

In social media, the THINK acronym has gained popularity. It was originally created to reduce online bullying, but we can use it to help us in our communication with others to increase our RelateAbility. Before responding to an email, text, or even in-person conversation, ask yourself if what you are going to say is True, Helpful, Inspiring, Necessary, and Kind.

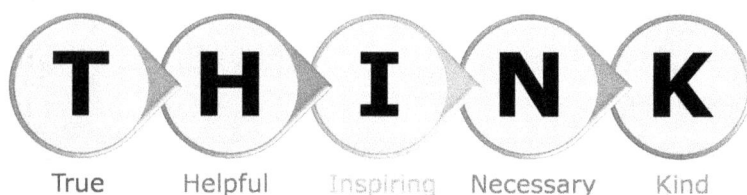

True   Helpful   Inspiring   Necessary   Kind

It takes only a few seconds to pause, THINK, and Respond Rationally. Emotions are important and should be validated. However, RelateAbility is our common goal and priority in making work life better.

> Improving RelateAbility is our Personal Choice. It is only when we choose to focus on creating, building, and maintaining better relationships, that we become our best selves.

RelateAbility and Trust

Understanding Trust

Trust is foundational to building and maintaining good relationships. Research shows that trust is essential to productive teams, and the lack of trust leads to team dysfunction. Building Trust is also a critical competency in Leadership research.

Trust takes time to earn and can be broken in a moment. If trust is broken, trying to rebuild that trust will take more focus, time, and effort than it does to initially build it. Having an understanding of trust and a common language to discuss trust in our relationships will help in bettering our RelateAbility.

When broken down to its core, trust is all about expectations. In any relationship, be it personal or professional, we each create expectations of the other person or team.

We believe these expectations are mutually understood by everyone. However, this is often not the case. Missed expectations cause trust to be tarnished, and if not met over time, they cause trust to transition to active distrust.

Creating a Common Language

We tend to grow and develop most when we are able to communicate in a common language. To help facilitate constructive dialog with others on trust, let's look at six components that make up the Trust Triangle.

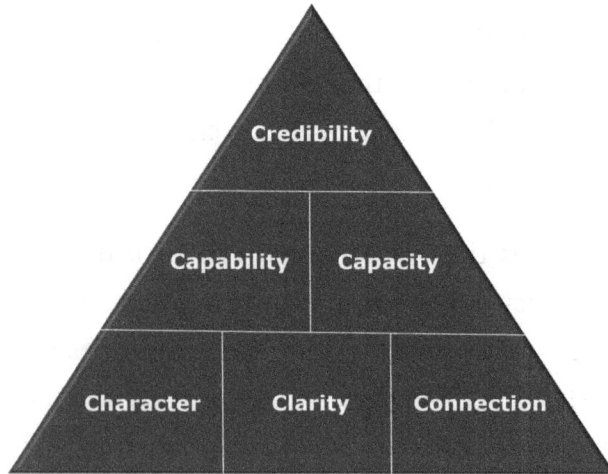

© Wade A. McNair. Used with Permission.

Foundational Level

At the foundational level, the components of trust have the most common areas of misperception and misunderstanding. They are:

- **Character** – the intent of the individual to positively influence, do the right thing, and meet expectations.

- **Clarity** – understanding the context and situation and effectively communicating expectations.

- **Connection** – rapport, relationship, and the desire to positively influence and meet expectations.

Middle Level

At the middle level, the components of trust are specific to the situation and are more easily identified. They are:

- **Capability** – skills and abilities one needs to meet the expectations.

- **Capacity** – the bandwidth, the resources (time, energy, etc.) to meet expectations.

Top Level

At the top level is the component of trust that is most visible. It is on this level that trust is most commonly judged. It is also on this level that we have the greatest opportunity to build trust and experience immediate development and growth.

- **Credibility** – the experience of someone doing what they said they would do, the act of meeting expectations.

Productive Conversations

We can't just say we don't trust someone. We need to understand why trust is low. We need to ask for feedback to determine what we are doing or saying that is causing trust to be eroded. Productive conversations on Trust begin at the top of the Trust Triangle, asking if we "do what we say we will do." From there, we explore each component, asking questions about the perspective of others.

For each component, we should seek understanding of specific situations, the behaviors that were demonstrated, and the resulting impact of those behaviors on the relationship. Conversely, we should use this same process when giving feedback to others using the Trust Triangle.

Consider the following questions when evaluating the trust you place in others, and the trust others place in you:

- **Credibility** – Have I been doing what I said I would do? When they say they are going to do something, do they follow through?

- **Capability** – Do I have the skills and abilities to meet the expectations set before me? Do they have the skills and abilities to meet my expectations?

- **Capacity** – Do I have the time, energy, and bandwidth to meet the expectations set before me? Do they have the time, energy, and bandwidth to meet the expectations I set for them?

- **Clarity** – Do I have a full understanding of the expectations set before me, including context and urgency? Have I effectively communicated my expectations for others, including context and urgency?

- **Character** – Am I bringing to the relationship the desire to positively influence, and do I expect the best from others? Do I believe they are showing an intent to positively influence and do the right thing in order to meet my expectations?

- **Connection** – Do I actively seek to understand others and build relationships founded on dignity, compassion, integrity, and respect? Do I create an environment where others feel connected to the mission, vision, and values of the team? Are my team members treating themselves and each other with dignity, compassion, integrity, and respect?

When we challenge ourselves to ask these tough questions, we create an opportunity to evaluate our own actions and behaviors and their impact on others. When we are willing to be vulnerable with others and ask them to answer these questions about us, we are given the opportunity to see ourselves from the perspective of others.

The Trust Triangle creates a common language and is a tool to better understand the causes of many Trust issues. It takes time to build and maintain Trust, a willingness to acknowledge that Trust is an issue, and purposeful effort to overcome the gap between expectations and reality.

TeamRelate and Dayforce HCM

Dayforce Human Capital Management (HCM) is a solution focused on talent management provided by Ceridian, a global leader in business systems.

RelateAbility is a skill that can be learned by anyone and is enhanced with Dayforce TeamRelate. We empower RelateAbility by using the behavior science of TeamRelate, combined with personalized content and individual check-ins, to help managers and employees understand their Communication Style, Core Convictions, and how to best communicate with others in the workplace. Better teams are achieved when team members gain a deeper understanding of their similarities, differences, do's and don'ts, and how to build and maintain more effective relationships.

Using TeamRelate, Dayforce HCM helps ignite teams through enhanced communication. Dayforce HCM captures this information for each of your employees and candidates by providing a brief survey and through daily engagement check-ins. The check-in functionality enables your employees to indicate their engagement levels based on their levels of Stress, Emotion, Energy, Activity, and their Day-at-Work. Check-ins provide important cues to an individual's manager and peers for how to structure their interactions with the individual.

Using TeamRelate, Dayforce HCM empowers people's development through personalized coaching. Dayforce HCM enables organizations to create a culture of development, helping people take a more active role in their own development. Managers are provided practical personalized coaching designed to offer insight and a better understanding of how best to communicate with that team member.

Using TeamRelate, Dayforce HCM enables continuous performance development. Recognizing that different personalities require different ways of receiving feedback, Dayforce HCM uses employee TeamRelate profiles to provide managers with personalized coaching on how to motivate the employee in question.

By providing managers with practical, personalized coaching to use in daily interactions with their teams, performance development becomes an ongoing experience rather than a yearly event.

By combining Communication Styles, Core Convictions, check-ins, and coaching content, Dayforce TeamRelate provides a powerful technology tool to help build trust through understanding, increasing RelateAbility and maximizing the effectiveness of teams in the workplace.

For more information on Dayforce using TeamRelate, contact:

1.800.729.7655

http://www.ceridian.com/human-capital-management/index.html

Supporting Research

RelateAbility/Emotional Intelligence

Barrick, M. R., Stewart, G. L., Neubert, M. J., & Mount, M. K. (1998). Relating member ability and personality to work-team processes and team effectiveness. *Journal of Applied Psychology*, 83(3), 377.

Bradberry, T., & Greaves, J. (2009). *Emotional intelligence 2.0.* San Diego: TalentSmart.

Goleman, D. (1995). *Emotional Intelligence: Why It Can Matter More Than IQ.* New York: Bantam Books.

Goleman, D. (1998). *Working with Emotional Intelligence.* New York: Bantam Books.

Jordan, P. J., Ashkanasy, N. M., Härtel, C. E., & Hooper, G. S. (2002). Workgroup Emotional Intelligence: Scale development and Relationship to Team Process Effectiveness and Goal Focus. *Human Resource Management Review*, 12(2), 195-214.

Melita Prati, L., Douglas, C., Ferris, G. R., Ammeter, A. P., & Buckley, M. R. (2003). Emotional Intelligence, Leadership Effectiveness, and

Team Outcomes. *The International Journal of Organizational Analysis,* 11(1), 21-40.

Offermann, L. R., Bailey, J. R., Vasilopoulos, N. L., Seal, C., & Sass, M. (2004). The Relative Contribution of Emotional Competence and Cognitive Ability to Individual and Team Performance. *Human Performance,* 17(2), 219-243.

Stubbs Koman, E., & Wolff, S. B. (2008). Emotional Intelligence Competencies in the Team and Team Leader: A Multi-Level Examination of the Impact of Emotional Intelligence on Team Performance. *Journal of Management Development,* 27(1), 55-75.

Rapisarda, B. A. (2002). The Impact of Emotional Intelligence on Work Team Cohesiveness and Performance. *The International Journal of Organizational Analysis,* 10(4), 363-379.

Personality Defined

McAdams, D.P. & Olson, B.D. (2010). Personality Development: Continuity and Change Over the Life Course. *Annual Review of Psychology,* 61, 517–42. doi:10.1146/annurev.psych.093008.100507.

Mischel, W., Shoda, Y., & Smith, R. E. (2004). *Introduction to Personality: Toward an Integration.* New York: John Wiley & Sons.

Winnie, J.F., & Gittinger, J.W. (1973). An Introduction to the Personality Assessment System. *Journal of Clinical Psychology, Monograph Supplement*, 38, 1-68.

Jeronimus, B. F., Riese, H., Sanderman, R., & Ormel, J. (2014). Mutual Reinforcement Between Neuroticism and Life Experiences: A Five-Wave, 16-Year Study to Test Reciprocal Causation. *Journal of Personality and Social Psychology*, 107(4), 751–64. doi:10.1037/a0037009. PMID 25111305.

Allport, Gordon W. (1961) *Pattern and Growth in Personality*. New York: Holy, Rinehart & Wilson.

Murray, Henry Alexander. (1938). *Explorations in Personality*. Oxford, England: Oxford Univ. Press.

Hall, Calvin S., & Lindzey, Gardner. (1957). *Theories of Personality*. Hoboken, NJ: Wiley.

Nature and Nurture

Hogben, Lancelot. (1933). *Nature and Nurture*. Great Britain: Unwin Brothers Ltd.

Owen, Michael J. (2006). Genes and Behavior: Nature-Nurture Interplay Explained. *The British Journal of Psychiatry*, 189(2), 192-193. 10.1192/bjp.189.2.192.

Esposito, E. A., Grigorenko, E.L., & Sternberg, R. J. (2011). The Nature-Nurture Issue (An Illustration Using Behaviour-Genetic Research on Cognitive Development). *In Alan Slater, & Gavin Bremner (eds.) An Introduction to Developmental Psychology: Second Edition*, BPS Blackwell.

Dusheck, Jennie. (2002). The Interpretation of Genes. *Natural History J,* 111, 52.

Ridley, M. (2003). *Nature via Nurture: Genes, Experience, & What Makes Us Human.* Harper Collins. New York: Harper Collins ISBN 1-84114-745-7.

Pinker, Steven. (2002). *The Blank Slate: The Modern Denial of Human Nature.* Viking; First edition. New York: Viking ISBN 978-0670031511.

Weiss, A., Bates TC, & Luciano M. (2008). Happiness is a personal(ity) thing: the genetics of personality and well-being in a representative sample. *Psychological Science,* 19(3), 205–10. doi:10.1111/j.1467-9280.2008.02068.x. PMID 18315789. Retrieved 2011-07-20.

Powledge, Tabitha M. (2011). Behavioral Epigenetics: How Nurture Shapes Nature. *BioScience,* 61(8), 588–592. doi:10.1525/bio.2011.61.8.4.

Focus and Function - Task vs. Relationship and Internal vs. External

Forsyth, Donelson R. (2010). *Group Dynamics* (5th ed.). Belmont, CA: Wadsworth Cengage Learning, 253.

Griffin, Ronald J., & Ebert, Ricky W. (2010). *Business Essentials* (8th ed.). Upper Saddle River, NJ: Prentice Hall, 135–136.

Anzalone, Chris. Differences between Task-Oriented Leaders & Relational-Oriented Leaders. *Demand Media*. Retrieved 3 November 2012.

Burke, C. Shawn, Stagl, Kevin C., Klein, Cameron, Goodwin, Gerald F., Salas, Eduardo, & Halpin, Stanley M. (2006). What type of leadership behaviors are functional in teams? A meta-analysis. *The Leadership Quarterly*, 17, 288–307.

Moghaddam, Afsane Zamani, Ghanbari, Ali, & Hosseinzadeh, Allahverdi. (2011). Relationship between the Leadership Method and Self Efficacy of the Staff. *American Journal of Scientific Research* 40, 160–172.

Arana, Jose M., Chambel, M. Jose, Curral, Luis, & Tabernero, Carmen. (2009). The role of task-oriented versus relationship-oriented leadership on normative contract and group performance. *Social Behavior and Personality: An International Journal*, 37(10), 1391. doi:10.2224/sbp.2009.37.10.1391.

Parish, T. S., & Parish, J. G. (2016). A comparison of external and internal control psychology. *International Journal of Choice Theory and Reality Therapy*, 35(2), 10-13.

Martin, C. R. (2007). Looking at type: the fundamentals. Gainesville, FL: Center for Applications of Psychological Type.

Helgoe, Laurie (2008). *Introvert Power: Why Your Inner Life is Your Hidden Strength*. Naperville, Illinois: Sourcebooks, Inc.

Personality - Background and History

Zhang, H. (1988), PSYCHOLOGICAL MEASUREMENT IN CHINA. *International Journal of Psychology*, 23, 101–117. doi:10.1080/00207598808247755.

Goldstein, G., & Hersen, M. (2007). *Handbook of Psychological Assessment*. Amsterdam: Elsevier.

Highfield, R., Wiseman, R., & Jenkins, R. (2009) How your looks betray your personality. *New Scientist*, 2695. http://bit.ly/2tWGNaj.

Roy Porter. (2003). Marginalized practices. *The Cambridge History of Science: Eighteenth-Century Science*, 4 (illustrated ed.). Cambridge University Press. pp. 495–497.

Myers, Isabel Briggs with Myers, Peter B. (1995). *Gifts Differing: Understanding Personality Type*. Mountain View, California: Davies-Black Publishing.

Bradberry, T. (2009). *Self-Awareness*. Penguin.

Sharp, Daryl. (1987). *Personality Types: Jung's Model of Typology*. Toronto, Canada: Inner City Books.

Marston, William M. (1928). *Emotions of Normal People*. K. Paul, Trench, Trubner & Co. Ltd.

Keirsey, David. (1998). *Please Understand Me II: Temperament, Character, Intelligence* (1st ed.). Prometheus Nemesis Book Co.

Pittenger, David J. (1993). Measuring the MBTI...And Coming Up Short. *Journal of Career Planning and Employment*. 54(1), 48–52.

Briggs Myers, Isabel, & McCaulley, Mary H. (1985). *Manual: A Guide to the Development and Use of the Myers-Briggs Type Indicator* (2nd ed.). Palo Alto, California.

Snygg, Donald, Combs, Arthur W. (1949) *Individual Behavior: A New Frame of Reference for Psychology*. Harper.

Combs, Arthur W., & Snygg, Donald. (1959). *Individual Behavior: A Perceptual Approach to Behavior*. Harper.

John Levi Martin. (2003). What Is Field Theory? *American Journal of Sociology*, 1, 1-49, 109. DOI: 10.1086/375201.

Social perception and phenomenal causality. *Heider, F. Psychological Review*, 51(6), Nov 1944, 358-374. http://bit.ly/2ubTNUK.

Combs, A. W., & Snygg, D. (1949). A New Frame of Reference for Psychology. New York: Harper and Brothers.

Rogers, Carl. (1953). *Client-centered therapy: Its current practice, implications and theory*. London: Constable.

Barry, P. (2002). *Mental Health and Mental Illness*. (7th ed.) New York: Lippincott.

Rogers, Carl. (1959). A theory of therapy, personality relationships as developed in the client-centered framework. *In (Ed.) S. Koch. Psychology: A Study of a Science*, 3, 184-256.

Cattell, R. B. (1978). *The Use of Factor Analysis in Behavioral and Life Sciences*. New York: Plenum.

Cattell, R. B. & Schuerger, J. M. (1978). *Personality Theory in Action: Handbook for the Objective-Analytic (O-A) Test Kit*. Champaign, IL: IPAT.

Cattell, R. B. & Sells, S. B. (1974). *The Clinical Analysis Questionnaire*. Champaign, IL: IPAT.

Conn, S. R. & Rieke, M. L. (1994). *The 16PF Fifth Edition Technical Manual*. Champaign, IL: IPAT.

Russell, M. T., & Karol, D. L. (1994) *The 16PF Fifth Edition Administrator's Manual*. Champaign, IL: IPAT.

Tupes, E. C., & Christal, R. E. (1961). Recurrent personality factors based on trait ratings. *USAF ASD Tech. Rep.* No. 61-97.

Goldberg, L. R. (1993). The structure of phenotypic personality traits. *American Psychologist*, 48, 26–34. doi:10.1037/0003-066x.48.1.26. PMID 8427480.

Toegel, G., & Barsoux, J. L. (2012). How to become a better leader. *MIT Sloan Management Review*, 53(3), 51–60.

DeYoung, C. G., Quilty, L. C., & Peterson, J. B. (2007). Between facets and domain: 10 aspects of the Big Five. *Journal of Personality and Social Psychology*, 93, 880–896.

Rothmann, S., & Coetzer, E. P. (2003). The big five personality dimensions and job performance. *SA Journal of Industrial Psychology*, 29, 68-74. doi:10.4102/sajip.v29i1.88. Retrieved 27 June 2013.

Digman, J. M. (1990). Personality structure: Emergence of the five-factor model. *Annual Review of Psychology*, 41, 417–440. doi:10.1146/annurev.ps.41.020190.002221.

Digman, J. M. (1989). Five robust trait dimensions: Development, stability, and utility. *Journal of Personality*, 57(2), 195–214. doi:10.1111/j.1467-6494.1989.tb00480.x. PMID 2671337.

Goldberg, L.R. (2001). Analyses of Digman's child-personality data: Derivation of Big Five Factor Scores from each of six samples. *Journal of Personality*, 69, 709–743. doi:10.1111/1467-6494.695161.

Block, J. (1995). Going beyond the five factors given: Rejoinder to Costa and McCrae and Goldberg and Saucier. *Psychological Bulletin*, 117, 226–229. doi:10.1037/0033-2909.117.2.226.

Communication Styles - Focus and Function/Internal and External

Forsyth, Donelson R. (2010). *Group Dynamics* (pp. 253.) (5th ed.) Belmont, CA: Wadsworth Cengage Learning. ISBN 9780495599524.

Griffin, Ronald J., & Ebert, Ricky W. (2010). *Business Essentials*, 8, 135–136. Upper Saddle River, NJ: Prentice Hall. ISBN 0-13-705349-5.

Anzalone, C. (2012). Differences Between Task-Oriented Leaders & Relational-Oriented Leaders. Retrieved July 27, 2017, from http://bit.ly/2vaJdlB.

Burke, C. Shawn, Stagl, Kevin C., Klein, Cameron, Goodwin, Gerald F., Salas, Eduardo, & Halpin, Stanley M. (2006). What type of leadership behaviors are functional in teams? A meta-analysis. *The Leadership Quarterly*, 17, 288–307.

Moghaddam, Afsane Zamani, Ghanbari, Ali, & Hosseinzadeh, Allah-verdi. (2011). Relationship between the Leadership Method and Self Efficacy of the Staff. *American Journal of Scientific Research*, 40, 160–172.

Arana, Jose M., Chambel, M. Jose, Curral, Luis, & Tabernero, Carmen. (2009). The role of task-oriented versus relationship-oriented leadership on normative contract and group performance. *Social Behavior and Personality: An International Journal*, 37(10), 1391. doi:10.2224/sbp.2009.37.10.1391.

Parish, T. S., & Parish, J. G. (2016). A comparison of external and internal control psychology. *International Journal of Choice Theory And Reality Therapy*, 35(2), 10-13.

Martin, C. R. (2007). Looking at type: the fundamentals. Gainesville, FL: Center for Applications of Psychological Type.

Helgoe, Laurie. (2008). *Introvert Power: Why Your Inner Life is Your Hidden Strength*. Naperville, Illinois: Sourcebooks, Inc.

Values – Background and History

Rokeach, Milton. (1973). *The Nature of Human Values*. New York: Free Press.

Allport, G. W., P. E. Vernon, & Lindsey, G. (1960). *A Study of Values*. Boston: Houghton Mifflin.

Ball-Rokeach, Sandra, & Loges, William E. (1992). Value Theory and Research. In E. F. Borgatta and M. L. Borgatta, eds., *Encyclopedia of Sociology*, 1. New York: MacMillan.

Blake, Judith, & Davis, K. (1964). Norms, Values and Sanctions. pp 456-485 in R. F. L. Faris ed. *Handbook of Modern Sociology*. Chicago. Rand McNally.

Grube, Joel W., Mayton, Daniel M., & Ball Rokeach, Sandra. (1994). Inducing Change in Values, Attitudes, and Behaviors: Belief System Theory and the Method of Value Self-Confrontation. *Journal of Social Issues*, 50, 153-174.

Inglehart, Ronald. (1990). *Culture Shift in Advanced Industrial Society*. Princeton, N.J: Princeton University Press.

Kagitcibasi, Cigdem. (1997). Individualism and Collectivism. In J.W. Berry, M. H. Segall, and C. Kagitcibasi, eds. *Handbook of Cross-Cultural Psychology*, 3. Boston: Allyn and Bacon.

Kluckhohn, Clyde. (1951). Values and Value Orientation in the Theory of Action. In T. Parsons and E. A. Shils, eds., Toward a General Theory of Action. Cambridge, Massachusetts: Harvard University Press.

Kuhn, M. H., & McPartland, R. (1954). An Empirical Investigation of Self-Attitudes. *American Sociological Review*, 19, 68-76.

Messick, David M., & McClintock, Charles G. (1968). Motivational Bases of Choice in Experimental Games. *Journal of Experimental Social Psychology*, 4, 1-25.

Schwartz, Shalom H. (1990). Individualism-Collectivism: Critique and Proposed Refinements. *Journal of Cultural Psychology*, 21, 139-157.

Schwartz, Shalom H. (1992). Universals in the Content and Structure of Values: Theoretical Advances and Empirical Tests in 20 Countries. *Advances in Experimental Social Psychology*, 25, 1-65.

Schwartz, Shalom H. (1996). Value Priorities and Behavior: Applying a Theory of Integrated Value Systems, In C. Seligman, J. M. Olson, and M. P. Zanna, eds., *The Psychology of Values: The Ontario Symposium*, 8. Mahwah, N.J.: Erlbaum.

Singelis, T., Triandis, H. C., Bhawuk, D. S., & Gelfand, M. (1995). Horizontal and Vertical Dimension of Individualism and Collectivism: A Theoretical and Measurement Refinement. *Cross-Cultural Research*, 29, 240-275.

Spates, James L. (1983). The Sociology of Values. *Annual Review of Sociology*, 9, 27-49.

Smith, Peter B. & Schwartz, Shalom. (1997). Values, In W. Berry, M. H. Segall, and C. Kagitcibasi, eds., *Handbook of Cross-Cultural Psychology*, 3. Boston: Allyn and Bacon.

Liebrand, Wim B. G. (1986). The Ubiquity of Social Values in Social Dilemmas. In H. A. M. Wilke, D. M. Messick, and C. G. Rutte, eds., Experimental Social Dilemmas. Frankfurt: Verlag Peter Lang.

TeamRelate Core Convictions/ABCD

Schwartz, S. H. (2012). An Overview of the Schwartz Theory of Basic Values. *Online Readings in Psychology and Culture*, 2(1). http://bit.ly/2foAGvb.

Schwartz, S. H., & Bardi, A. (1997). Influences of Adaptation to Communist Rule on Value Priorities in Eastern Europe. *Political Psychology*, 18, 385-410. http://bit.ly/2uN68SQ.

Schwartz, S. H., Melech, G., Lehmann, A., Burgess, S., & Harris, M. (2001). Extending the cross-cultural validity of the theory of basic human values with a different method of measurement. *Journal of Cross-Cultural Psychology*, 32, 519-542. http://bit.ly/2tR4Rap.

Schwartz, S. H. (1994). Are there universal aspects in the content and structure of values?

Journal of Social Issues, 50, 19-45. http://bit.ly/2vf3PbV.

Lonner, W. J. (1980). The search for psychological universals. In H. C. Triandis & W. W.

Lambert (Eds.), *Handbook of cross-cultural psychology. Perspectives*, 1,

143-204. Boston, MA: Allyn & Bacon.

Leung, K., & Bond, M. H. (2004). Social axioms: A model of social beliefs in multi-cultural perspective. In M. P. Zanna (Ed.), *Advances in
Experimental Social Psychology*,

36, 119-197. San Diego, CA: Academic Press. http://bit.ly/2uciaBX.

Bilsky, W., Janik, M., & Schwartz, S. H. (2011). The structural organization of human values – Evidence from three rounds of the European
Social Survey (ESS). *Journal of Cross-Cultural Psychology*, 42, 759-776.
http://bit.ly/2tRdLF9.

Kluckhohn, C. (1951). Values and value-orientations in the theory of
action: An exploration in definition and classification. In T. Parsons &
E. Shils (Eds.), Toward a general theory of action (pp. 388-433). Cambridge, MA: Harvard University Press.

Oishi, S., Schimmack, U., Diener, E., & Suh, E. (1998). The measurement of values and individualism-collectivism. *Personality and Social
Psychology Bulletin*, 24, 1177-1189. http://bit.ly/2vluSTQ.

Schwartz, S. H., & Boehnke, K. (2004). Evaluating the structure of human values with confirmatory factor analysis. *Journal of Research in
Personality*, 38, 230-255. http://bit.ly/2ucua66.

Smith, P. B., & Schwartz, S. H. (1997). Values. In J. W. Berry, M. H.
Segall, & C. Kagitcibasi (Eds.), *Handbook of Cross-Cultural Psychology*,
2nd ed., Vol. 3, (pp. 77-118). Boston, MA: Allyn & Bacon.

RelateAbility and Engagement

Crooks, Claire V. et al. (2010). Strengths-based programming for First Nations youth in schools: Building engagement through healthy relationships and leadership skills. *International Journal of Mental Health and Addiction*, 8(2), 160-173.

Corporate Leadership Council. (2004). *Driving Performance and Retention Through Employee Engagement.* Washington, DC: Corporate Executive Board.

Leithwood, Kenneth, & Jantzi, Doris. (2000). The effects of transformational leadership on organizational conditions and student engagement with school. *Journal of Educational Administration*, 38(2), 112-129.

Zhang, Xiaomeng, & Bartol, Kathryn M. (2010). Linking empowering leadership and employee creativity: The influence of psychological empowerment, intrinsic motivation, and creative process engagement. *Academy of Management Journal*, 53(1), 107-128.

Macey, William H., & Schneider, Benjamin. (2008). The meaning of employee engagement. *Industrial and Organizational Psychology*, 1(1), 3-30.

Schaufeli, Wilmar B., Taris, Toon W., & Van Rhenen, Willem. (2008). Workaholism, burnout, and work engagement: three of a kind or three different kinds of employee well-being?. *Applied Psychology*, 57(2), 173-203.

Thomas, Kenneth Wayne. (2009). *Intrinsic Motivation at Work: What Really Drives Employee Engagement.* Berrett-Koehler Publishers.

Markos, Solomon, & Sridevi, M. Sandhya. (2010). Employee engagement: The key to improving performance. *International Journal of Business and Management, 5*(12), 89-96.

Gruman, Jamie A., & Saks, Alan M. (2011). Performance management and employee engagement. *Human Resource Management Review, 21*(2), 123-136.

Salanova, Marisa, Agut , Sonia, & Peiró, José María. (2005). Linking organizational resources and work engagement to employee performance and customer loyalty: the mediation of service climate. *Journal of applied Psychology, 90*(6), 1217.

Shaw, Kieron. (2005). An engagement strategy process for communicators. *Strategic Communication Management, 9*(3), 26.

Mishra, Karen, Lois Boynton, & Aneil Mishra. (2014). Driving employee engagement: The expanded role of internal communications. *International Journal of Business Communication, 51*(2), 183-202.

RelateAbility in Conflict

Afzalur Rahim, M. (2002) Toward a Theory of Managing Organizational Conflict. *International Journal of Conflict Management, 13*(3), 206-235.

Ulrich-Lai, Yvonne M., & Herman, James P. (2017). Neural Regulation of Endocrine and Autonomic Stress Responses. *Nature reviews: Neuroscience*, 10(6), 397–409. doi:10.1038/nrn2647. ISSN 1471-003X.

Segerstrom, Suzanne C., & Miller, Gregory E. (2017). Psychological Stress and the Human Immune System: A Meta-Analytic Study of 30 Years of Inquiry. *Psychological Bulletin*, 130(4), 601–630. doi:10.1037/0033-2909.130.4.601. ISSN 0033-2909.

Stephens, Mary Ann C., & Wand, Gary. (2012). Stress and the HPA Axis. *Alcohol Research: Current Reviews*, 34(4), 468–483. ISSN 2168-3492.

Friedman, Raymond A., et al. (2000). What goes around comes around: The impact of personal conflict style on work conflict and stress. *International Journal of Conflict Management*, 11(1), 32-55.

Coverman, Shelley. (1989). Role overload, role conflict, and stress: Addressing consequences of multiple role demands. *Social Forces*, 965-982.

RelateAbility and Trust

Brown, C. Brene. (2012). *The Power of Vulnerability*. Sounds True.

Fukuyama, Francis. (1995). *Trust: The Social Virtues and the Creation of Prosperity*. New York: Free Press.

Kramer, Roderick M., & Tyler, Tom R. (1996). *Trust in Organizations: Frontiers of Theory and Research*. Sage.

McKnight, D. H., & Chervany, N. L. (1996). The Meanings of Trust. Carlson School of Management, University of Minnesota.

Peters, Richard G., Covello, Vincent T., & McCallum, David B. (1997). The determinants of trust and credibility in environmental risk communication: An empirical study. *Risk Analysis*, 17(1), 43-54.

Renn, Ortwin, & Levine, Debra. (1991). *Credibility and Trust in Risk Communication. Communicating Risks to the Public.* Springer Netherlands.

Denhardt, Robert B. (2002). Trust as capacity: The role of integrity and responsiveness. *Public Organization Review*, 2(1), 65-76.

Cosner, Shelby. (2009). Building organizational capacity through trust. *Educational Administration Quarterly*, 45(2), 248-291.

Delgado, Mauricio R., Frank, Robert H., & Phelps, Elisabeth A. (2005). Perceptions of moral character modulate the neural systems of reward during the trust game. *Nature Neuroscience*, 8(11), 1611-1618.

Lahno, Bernd. (2001). On the emotional character of trust. *Ethical Theory and Moral Practice*, 4(2), 171-189.

Clark, Murray C., & Payne, Roy L. (2006). Character-Based Determinants of Trust in Leaders. *Risk Analysis*, 26(5), 1161-1173.

Lapointe, Émilie, Vandenberghe, Christian, & Boudrias, Jean-Sébastien. (2014). Organizational socialization tactics and newcomer adjustment: The mediating role of role clarity and affect-based trust relationships. *Journal of Occupational and Organizational Psychology,* 87(3), 599-624.

Randall, Wesley S., Gravier, Michael J., & Prybutok, Victor R. (2011). Connection, trust, and commitment: dimensions of co-creation?. *Journal of Strategic Marketing,* 19(01), 3-24.

Tinsley, D.B. (1996), Trust plus capabilities. *The Academy of Management Review,* 21(2), 335-7.

Blaze, Matt, Feigenbaum, Joan, & Lacy, Jack. Decentralized trust management. Security and Privacy, 1996. Proceedings., 1996 IEEE Symposium on. IEEE, 1996.

Validity and Reliability of TeamRelate Survey (2016)

Submitted to: Ceridian, Inc.

Submitted by:
Caitlin Carney, Yaksh Patel, & Dr. Brian J. O'Leary
The University of Tennessee at Chattanooga

Submission date: March 3, 2016

Executive Summary

Reliability is a critical component of the scale validation process. Building on a previous study which demonstrated the convergent and discriminant validity of the *Worktraits*

Compatibility Assessment (*WCA*, an earlier version of *TeamRelate*) relative to existing measures of personality (Weathington, Nordbrock, & Manier, 2012), the present study examined two types of reliability for the *TeamRelate Communication Styles* (Director, Encourager, Facilitator, & Tracker) and *Core Convictions* (Ambition, Belief, Compassion, & Discipline): 1) *internal consistency reliability*, measured with Cronbach's alpha (α), which shows how well items for each trait focus on the same construct, and 2) *test-retest reliability*, or how consistent the measurement results are within individuals over time.

We completed the analysis of internal consistency reliability (Cronbach's alpha) on a Time 1 sample of Ceridian employees (*n*=1305) and found acceptable alpha levels for all *TeamRelate* traits ($\alpha > .70$, Nunnally, 1978) with the exception of the Facilitator trait ($\alpha = .625$). On the basis of these results, we modified the Facilitator trait, and in February 2016, collected *TeamRelate* data from a sample of Ceridian employees (*n* = 154), including a subsample of those who participated in the Time 1 study (*n* = 103). Time 2 results found all alphas in the acceptable range, with a significant improvement in the Facilitator trait ($\alpha = .860$). Results for the comparison group for Times 1 and 2 also revealed good test-retest reliability for individual traits. Overall, these results provide a basis from which to replicate Weathington's (2011) validation study on the *WCA*, which found significant positive relationships between

WCA components and performance-related variables, including peer and supervisory ratings of individual performance.

Introduction

In October of 2015, Ted Malley of Ceridian, Inc. requested that we analyze the *TeamRelate* traits using data collected from Ceridian employees ($n = 1305$), with an emphasis on the reliability of the measures of the eight traits assessed in the instrument. Reliability is a critical component of the validation process.

Construct Validity of the TeamRelate Subscales

Employers need an efficient and standardized method of determining employee characteristics to be used as part of valid job analysis, selection and recruitment procedures, performance evaluation, and team/organizational development. Before an assessment can be validated for a particular use, however, it is critical that we demonstrate two types of reliability: 1) *internal consistency* reliability, and 2) *test-retest* reliability. Internal consistency reliability reflects the degree to which the items in a scale measure the same underlying construct (Cortina, 1993), whereas test-retest reliability measures the consistency of the results within the individual across time. Reliability is a necessary but not sufficient component of validity. Test-retest relia-bility is particularly important within the context of the present study as *TeamRelate* taps into components of indi-vidual personality which are, by definition, *consistent* patterns of individual differences in thinking, feeling, and behaving (APA.org).

Purpose

The purpose of the present study is to:

- Examine the internal consistency reliability (Cronbach's alpha) of the eight *TeamRelate* traits to demonstrate that the items in each subscale meas-ure the same underlying construct.

- Examine test-retest reliability of the eight *TeamRelate* traits to demonstrate the consistency of the measure within an individual over time.

- Examine possible modification to the wording of individual items and the number of items included in each of the *TeamRelate* traits.

- Present a theoretical link of the *TeamRelate* traits to important organizational outcomes based on exist-ing empirical research, as a preliminary step in the validation process for the *TeamRelate* taxonomy.

Applicable Research Supporting Validity of TeamRelate

The use of individual characteristics to improve organi-zational performance has a long history in the study of

Industrial-Organizational (I-O) psychology. Previous studies by Weathington (2011) and Weathington et al. (2012) analyzing an earlier version of *TeamRelate* called the *Worktraits Compatibility Assessment (WCA)* identified important relationships between the *WCA* and other personality measures and variables related to organizational performance. Because of their common derivation, we can reasonably conclude that the *WCA* and *TeamRelate* have very similar psychometric properties; we will use this similarity to impute the validity of *TeamRelate* in anticipation of the completion of our reliability and validity studies of that instrument.

Convergent Validity Study - Weathington et al. (2012)

Weathington et al. (2012) performed analyses of the convergent and discriminant validity of the *WCA* against existing measures of personality, most notably the Big 5 personality measure (Barrick & Mount, 1991; Digman, 1990), whose relationship to direct and indirect indicators of organizational performance has received significant exploration in both academic and applied literature. The Big 5 includes:

- *Openness to Experience* – inquisitive, curious, adaptive, and able to resolve conflict.

- *Conscientiousness* – detail-oriented, well-organized, thoughtful, driven, finish what they start.

- *Extraversion* – energetic, passionate, outgoing, assertive, outspoken, and gregarious.

- *Agreeableness* – cooperative, conflict avoidant, altruistic, trusting, and helpful.

- *Neuroticism/Emotional Stability* – consistency in mood and emotional states.

Consistent with existing empirical research, the results obtained from a sample of 326 college undergraduates at a medium-sized regional public institution in the Southeast U.S. indicated several interesting relationships supporting the validity of the *WCA*, and indirectly, *TeamRelate*, for the prediction of variables related to organizational performance. Among these findings:

- Encourager (Communication Style) was significantly related to Extraversion (r = .594).

- Tracker (Communication Style) was significantly related to Conscientiousness (r = .490).

- Compassion (Core Conviction) was significantly related to Agreeableness (r = .618).

- Discipline (Core Conviction) was also significantly related to Conscientiousness (r = .418).

These results can be tied into existing research supporting relationships between variables relevant to the present study. For example, Barrick, Parks, and Mount (2005), in a sample of MBA students (n = 116), found significant positive correlations of Extraversion and Agreeableness with supervisory ratings of interpersonal performance (r = .24 and .20 respectively). This result provides support for the belief that *Encouragers* contribute to improved team cohesiveness and communication. Similarly, in a study of team performance in Chinese State Operated Enterprises (n = 562), Li, Zhou, Zhao, Zhang, and Zhang (2015) found a significant positive correlation between a team leader's Extraversion (r = .19) and Conscientiousness (r = .13) and both the team average of individual perceptions of collective efficacy (i.e. the belief in the team's ability to perform a specific task) and team performance. These results for Conscientiousness suggest a link between the *TeamRelate* Core Conviction of *Discipline* to team performance. In another team-based study, Monaghan et al. (2015) found a positive correlation between aggregate team Conscientiousness and performance by student project teams (r = .30), providing further support for the link of *Discipline* to team performance. Finally, in a meta-analysis of the existing Big 5 literature (n = 11), Mount, Barrick and Stewart (1998) examined the results of eleven studies and found significant positive correlations of Conscientiousness (r = .26) and Agreeableness (r = .21) with performance in jobs that involve personal interaction. Mount et al.'s (2005) results again bolster the discipline–team performance relationship, while also providing support for the Core

Conviction of Compassion as a predictor of team performance.

Criterion Validity Study – Weathington (2011)

Criterion validity provides support for the usefulness of a measure in predicting changes in an outcome of interest, in this case, variables directly or indirectly related to organizational performance. Weathington (2011) examined the validity of the *WCA* against self-report measures of various constructs related to performance with a sample of employees in a medium-sized service organization ($n = 164$) that included both supervisors and subordinates. Some of the more interesting results are:

- *Encourager* was positively related to peer and supervisor assessments of overall performance.

- *Facilitator* was positively related to peer assessments of decision making, tenacity, and overall performance.

- *Tracker* was positively related to peer evaluations of strategic decision making and supervisor evaluations of collaboration.

- *Belief* was positively related to peer evaluations of decision making, strategic decision making, and the ability to work well with others.

- *Compassion* was positively related to peer evaluations of decision making, strategic decision making, ability to work well with others, tenacity, collaboration, and overall performance. This facet was also positively related to supervisor evaluations of overall performance.

These results, combined with those of Weathington et al. (2012) and existing empirical research, provide a solid basis of support for further exploration of the reliability and validity of *TeamRelate*.

Method

We assessed internal consistency reliability using Cronbach's alpha analysis of data collected from 1305 Ceridian, Inc. employees in 2015 using the *TeamRelate* app. These participants completed the original 44 *TeamRelate* items.

To examine the stability of the internal consistency reliability of each across samples, as well as to measure the consistency of traits within individuals across time (*test-retest reliability*), in February 2016, most of these same Ceridian employees were asked to complete a modified version of *TeamRelate* using a web-based survey tool that included all of the original items and six additional items related to the *Facilitator* Communication Style. The sample to date includes 154 individuals, 103 of whom completed the survey in both Time 1 and Time 2.

Study Measure: TeamRelate Compatibility Assessment

The *TeamRelate* Compatibility Assessment (TCA) consists of 44 items scored on a seven point Likert-type scale that asks participants to evaluate each item on agreement from 1 = *Strongly Disagree* to 7 = *Strongly Agree*. There are no reverse-scored items. Items are then scored across four Communication Styles (individual traits) and four Core Convictions (individual values).

Descriptions for the four Communication Styles and four Core Convictions are presented below:

Core Convictions

Ambition: Ambition refers to the degree to which an individual is "forward-looking" and proactive in achieving significant goals.

Belief: Belief refers to the degree to which an individual trusts in and lives according to a predefined ethical system.

Compassion: Compassion refers to the degree to which an individual feels compelled to help those less fortunate.

Discipline: Discipline refers to the degree to which an individual is able to sustain focus and dedication toward the completion of a task or goal.

Communication Styles

Director: The Director trait refers to the degree to which an individual needs to be in charge or in control. It is the "Leader" trait.

Encourager: The Encourager trait refers to the degree to which someone is extroverted and socially oriented. It is the "People" trait.

Facilitator: The Facilitator trait refers to the degree to which an individual is helpful and supportive of others. It is the "Helper" trait.

Tracker: The Tracker trait refers to the degree to which an individual is careful about "tracking down" and taking care of details. It is the "Organizational" trait.

Results

Our two primary tasks for the present study were:

1. Determine *internal consistency reliability* by calculating Cronbach's alphas (α) for the eight *TeamRelate* traits using data collected in 2015 from a sample of 1305 Ceridian employees in Time 1 and 154 employees in Time 2.

2. Determine *test-retest reliability*, or the consistency of the traits within individuals over time.

Internal Consistency Reliability

Cronbach's alpha measures how well the items in a given scale "fit together" in focusing on a specific construct or, in the present case, a personal trait or characteristic. The more focused the scale items are on the specific trait under examination, for example, the *TeamRelate* Core Conviction of Ambition, the higher the Cronbach's alpha. Nunnally (1978) suggested that an α of .7 was adequate for initial scale development. The results of this analysis for the responses collected in Time 1 are presented in Table 1:

Table 1: Time 1 *TeamRelate* Cronbach's Alpha			
Core Convictions		**Communication Styles**	
Trait	**α**	**Trait**	**α**
Ambition	0.760	Director	0.736
Belief	0.801	Encourager	0.778
Compassion	0.876	Facilitator	0.625
Discipline	0.839	Tracker	0.748

These results show alphas above .7 for seven of the eight *TeamRelate* traits, with alphas approaching or in excess of .8 for the Core Convictions. Further, with the exception of Encourager (Weathington et al., 2012 α = .850 vs. .778), each of these alphas was higher than those found in an undergraduate student sample by Weathington et al. (2012) for the same traits in *WCA*.

To improve the alpha for the Facilitator trait, we modified the scale and included it in our Time 2 data collection in February 2016 for all traits. Time 2 results (n = 154) are presented in Table 2.

These results, combined with those in Table 1, demonstrate the stability of the foundational traits at two points in time, suggesting that they reflect the traits they intend to measure. Of particular note is the significantly improved alpha for the modified Facilitator trait in Time 2.

Table 2: Time 2 *TeamRelate* Cronbach's Alpha			
Core Convictions		Communication Styles	
Trait	α	Trait	A
Ambition	0.793	Director	0.704
Belief	0.846	Encourager	0.817
Compassion	0.866	Facilitator	0.860
Discipline	0.845	Tracker	0.774

Test-Retest Reliability

Test-retest reliability indicates the consistency of a trait within individuals over time. Comparative data for Time 1 and Time 2 were collected for a sample of 103 Ceridian employees who retook the modified *TeamRelate* instrument. To perform this analysis, we calculated individual trait scores for each of the eight traits and used these results to create Time 2 Trait Profiles for **Core Convictions** and **Communication Styles**, which we then compared to

Time 1 Trait Profiles. *TeamRelate* Trait Profiles are created by ranking the individual traits, including a Norm value that is equal to the average of the highest and lowest trait scores, to create a descriptor comprised of five letters followed by a number indicating the strength of the Norm value (>4.3=1, <4.3=2). This descriptor forms the basis for the *TeamRelate* analysis. For example, someone who is AB-NCD1 would have a dominant **Ambition** trait, followed closely by **Belief**, and a **Conviction Norm Value** greater than 4.3. Correlational analysis of the test-retest reliabilities of the *TeamRelate* traits are shown in Table 3:

Table 3: Test-retest Reliabilities for TeamRelate Traits							
Core Convictions				Communication Styles			
Ambition	Belief	Compassion	Discipline	Director	Encourager	Facilitator*	Tracker
76%	75%	66%	75%	72%	79%	76%	70%

*Note: To be consistent with Time 1, we calculated the Time 2 Facilitator trait using the original (unmodified) Facilitator items for this comparison.

For comparative purposes, results of a meta-analysis by Viswesvaran and Ones (2000) on the heavily researched Big 5 personality traits (Costa & McCrae, 1992) showed very similar results for both test-retest and internal consistency reliability, as summarized in Table 4 below:

Table 4: Results of Viswesvaran & Ones (2000) Meta-analysis of Big 5 Reliability		
Trait	Test-retest reliability	Internal consistency (α)
Emotional Stability	.75	.78
Extraversion	.76	.78
Openness to Experience	.71	.73
Agreeableness	.69	.75
Conscientiousness	.72	.78

These results are important, as the Big 5 personality traits are accepted as a reliable measure of personality and have been consistently linked to a variety of performance indicators. *TeamRelate* traits compares quite favorably with the results for the Big 5. Further, these results are impressive given the relatively long period (approximately six months) between the first and second administrations of the survey. As demonstrated in Weathington (2011), it is the individual traits that will be validated against outcomes of interest in future studies.

Results for Trait Profiles

While the individual trait *scores* show stability over time, as shown in Table 3 above, the stability of the *TeamRelate Trait Profiles* are more complex because they are formed by the ranking of each trait based on score magnitude to create the profile. With this in mind, we examined the consistency of the relative position of each trait within the calculated Trait Profile, where the highest score represents the respondent's dominant trait, while the second-ranked trait follows closely in importance. On this basis, our analysis again suggests that overall test-retest reliability is very good, with 91% (*n*=95) of respondents matching their first *or* second traits in their Trait Profiles on *both* the **Core Convictions** and **Communication Styles** from Time 1 to Time 2. More importantly, 65% (*n* = 68) of all respondents matched their dominant **Core Conviction** from Time 1 to Time 2, while over 75% (*n* = 79) matched their dominant **Communication Style**. A more detailed analysis revealed that 42% (*n* = 44) had exact matches for their two dominant **Core Convictions,** and 53% (*n* = 55) exactly matched their two dominant **Communication Styles**.

Because of the way the Trait Profiles are calculated, and because we did not measure moderating variables such as mood and stress, it not surprising that a relatively small number of respondents (16% for **Core Convictions** and 22% for **Communication Style**) had *exactly* the same Trait Profiles from Time 1 to Time 2.

Conclusion

The results of the present study provide support for the *internal consistency* reliability and *test-retest* reliability of the

TeamRelate traits, while suggesting the need to explore additional factors that moderate/impact the consistency of respondent answers. Additional insights into the factors affecting the stability of these traits over time is important, as the individual traits will be used in future validation studies linking *TeamRelate* to important performance-related variables.

This study provides a solid basis for future research upon which to continue to identify the many possible applications of the *TeamRelate* instrument moving forward.

References

Barrick, M. R., & Mount, M. K. (1991). The big five personality dimensions and job performance: a meta-analysis. *Personnel psychology*, 44(1), 1-26.

Barrick, M. R., Parks, L., & Mount, M. K. (2005). Self-monitoring as a moderator of the relationships between personality traits and performance. *Personnel Psychology*, 58, 745–767.

Cortina, J. (1993). What Is Coefficient Alpha? An Examination of Theory and Applications. *Journal of Applied Psychology*, 78(1), 98-104.

Costa, P. T., Jr., & McCrae, R. R. (1992). Four ways five factors are basic. *Personality and Individual Differences*, 13, 653-665.

Digman, J. M. (1990). Personality structure: Emergence of the five-factor model. *Annual Review of Psychology, 41,* 417-440.

Li, X., Zhou, M., Zhao, N., Zhang, S. & Zhang, J. (2015). Collective-efficacy as a mediator of the relationship of leaders' personality traits and team performance: A cross-level analysis. *International Journal of Psychology, 50,* 223–231.

Monaghan, C., Bizumic, B., Reynolds, K., Smithson, M., Johns-Boast, L., & Van Rooy, D. (2015). Performance of student software development teams: The influence of personality and identifying as team members. *European Journal of Engineering Education, 40*(1).

Mount, M. K., Barrick, M. R., & Stewart, G. L. (1998). Five-Factor Model of Personality and Performance in Jobs Involving Interpersonal Interactions. *Human Performance, 11*(2/3), 145-165.

Nunnally, J. C. (1978). *Psychometric Theory.* New York: McGraw Hill.

Viswesvaran, C., & Ones, D. S. (2000). Measurement error in "Big Five Factors" personality assessment: Reliability generalization across studies and measures. *Educational and Psychological Measurement, 60*(2), 224-235.

Weathington, B. L. (2011). Validation analysis: Worktraits Compatibility Assessment.

Weathington, B. L., Nordbrock, M., & Manier, A. (2012). Construct validity report: WorkTraits behavioral styles and Core Convictions.

What is your
TeamRelate Communication Style?

- Go to http://testdrive.teamrelate.com to participate in our COMPLIMENTARY survey.
- Using TeamRelate TestDrive, determine your primary Communication Style.
- Print out your profile and share your results!

www.ingramcontent.com/pod-product-compliance
Lightning Source LLC
Chambersburg PA
CBHW050729030426
42336CB00012B/1487